S0-BLR-751

Humor in Public Speaking

*H*umor

in *P*ublic *S*peaking

A Guide to Providing an Occasional Oasis in the Desert of Dreary Speeches and Clumsily Handled Speaking Programs

*J. E*dward *D*ay

West Nyack, N.Y.
Parker Publishing Company, Inc.

ALL RIGHTS RESERVED, INCLUDING THE RIGHT
TO REPRODUCE THIS BOOK, OR ANY PORTIONS
THEREOF, IN ANY FORM, EXCEPT FOR THE IN-
CLUSION OF BRIEF QUOTATIONS IN A REVIEW.

© 1965, by
Parker Publishing Company, Inc.
West Nyack, N.Y.

Library of Congress
Catalog Card No.: 65-18488

Third printing ...... August, 1966

PRINTED IN THE UNITED STATES OF AMERICA
44790—B&P

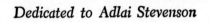

Dedicated to Adlai Stevenson

Introduction

This book has been written in the hope that it may help reduce by even a tiny fraction the enormous number of speeches that are heavy, dull, and soporific.

Its purpose is to explain why, when, and how to use humor in speeches—and when not to.

It is not a "joke book." Many stories and anecdotes are included as illustrations and examples. There are suggestions as to where to find good source material for humor and how to have a supply of stories to draw from.

Since humor alone will not make a successful speech and since a speech alone will not make a successful banquet, the book covers general aspects of putting on a well-received program.

Many a good speech is sabotaged by a poor introduction.

Many a good speaker never really gets off the ground because the occasio⌐ has been poorly planned and poorly managed.

Many a good speech is a flop because it is made to the wrong audience.

And, most often of all, many an audience goes away from a speaking event wondering why they came in the first place.

This book is dedicated to the proposition that successful affairs involving a speaking program don't just happen. They take thought, effort, imagination, and follow-through.

There are just a few big mistakes and omissions that are made in setting up luncheons, banquets, panels, and seminars—but these same mistakes and omissions are made over and over. People who would do the most careful checking before choosing a veterinarian or an upholsterer, will go along with giving the job of program chairman or toastmaster to any old body, just as long as he doesn't put up too much resistance.

Despite the competition of professional talent on radio and television, amateur speechmaking has proved to be an incredibly durable institution. In our increasingly affluent and highly gregarious society, more and more organizations are having more and more meetings to hear speeches.

Tax laws and company comptrollers combine to encourage "serious, educational" sessions at least part of the time at conventions. The overpowering American urge to keep informed has brought the ladies out of their bridge and canasta parties to hear lectures on comparative religion or the Malaysian problem. Another overpowering American urge, to get together for a few drinks and some socializing, is tempered by a Puritan ethic which says that there must be a worthwhile phase to the meeting—i.e., a speech—before adjournment.

Even in political speaking, television and radio have not reduced its frequency. They have only imposed a burdensome necessity for a different speech every time.

The purpose of this book is to highlight pitfalls and pointers for the program chairman, the publicity chairman, the toastmaster, and the speaker himself.

This book is not for those who are satisfied with dreariness, clumsiness, triteness, or pomposity. I am a firm believer that people are much more discriminating than we give them credit for—that they long for some sparkle and zest in the many speeches they listen to.

This book need not be read cover to cover. The chapter headings will lead you to your particular problem of the moment. However, if you do read the book straight through, you may sense that the reason I have written it is because I *like* speechmaking. It is my "art," just as the cello or amateur theatricals may be for certain others.

I have made hundreds of speeches—as a lawyer, as a member of Governor Adlai Stevenson's cabinet in Illinois, as a top business executive, as Postmaster General, as a charitable fund raiser, even as a naval officer. Many of the speeches have been entirely serious—to exhort or to explain or to challenge; some have been purely humorous; some have been political; some have been inspirational; some have been a combination.

I have also set up and supervised many speechmaking affairs, a large number of which have been devoted to sales promotion.

Scores of other times, while sitting as a helpless observer in the audience or at the head table, I have asked myself why those in charge had not done just a little bit of homework on the job they had to do.

This is not a Dale Carnegie book. It will not explain in four easy lessons how to emerge from a cocoon of shyness to become overnight a thundering Daniel Webster. (And anyway, Webster made many of his best speeches while under the influence, which I do not recommend.)

The theme of this book is that speech programing and speechmaking are both going to continue growing by leaps and bounds, and that experience and know-how in this field are negotiable.

Table

of Contents

1

*W*hy *U*se *H*umor?

Nearly everyone who makes a speech makes at least an attempt to start off with some humor. Instinctively we know it is a good idea.

There are several good reasons why use of humor in a speech is highly important.

First of all, it helps the speaker establish a connecting link with the audience. The listeners can tell very little about the personality and attitudes of a speaker from the introduction. In fact, if the introduction says that the speaker is a very important and brilliant man—even though most of the audience probably never heard of him—it may put the listeners on their guard. Are they going to be "lectured to" and talked down to by someone who is stuffy and impressed with his own importance?

Humor in a speech helps to tell the audience that the speaker does not take himself too seriously. A frequent device for achieving this is for the speaker to assure the audience that the introduction they have just heard is much too flattering.

Overcomes Flattery

After Lyndon Johnson became President he, of course, was only introduced by the accepted phrase:

"Ladies and gentlemen, I have the honor to present the President of the United States."

For it is definitely not proper to give any explanatory or biographical background when introducing the President.

But before he was President and after a flowery and highly complimentary introduction, Lyndon Johnson frequently would say:

"I wish my father and mother were alive so that they could have been here to hear that very fine introduction. My father would have enjoyed it—and my mother would have believed it."

At the American Bar Association Convention in New York in 1964, the Association President, Walter Craig, introduced Adlai Stevenson with glowing (and well-deserved) sentences about his distinguished public career, his part in establishing the United Nations, his service for five different Presidents, etc.

When Stevenson stood up he said:

"I was a little worried as Mr. Craig was giving

2

that wonderful introduction. I began to think he was going to introduce Benjamin Franklin."

Stevenson then went on, in his inimitable way, to establish himself with this largely conservative audience as a regular guy who did not take himself too seriously.

> I enjoy conventions. After these last few weeks at the United Nations struggling with Cyprus and Vietnam, I think even a national political convention might be a restful change. I well remember an incident at the 1956 Democratic Convention when I ran into a band of my followers parading in the convention hall. I was confronted with one especially large and enthusiastic woman. She was very obviously with child. And she was carrying a big sign that said:
>
> *Stevenson is the man.*

Earlier that evening while introducing the head table, President Craig made a memorable slip while trying to explain that a certain lady had had a great deal to do with the success of the meeting. He stumbled on the word "success":

"We are especially grateful to Mrs. —————— who has contributed so much to the sex of this meeting."

It could have been worse. Included among those he had just introduced was the dowager Marchioness of Reading, first woman member of the House of Lords, and Cardinal Spellman.

Back to "Why Use Humor?" To establish a rapport, a connecting link with the audience, to show them you are not a stuffed shirt.

Humor Relaxes

Humor at the beginning of a speech helps to loosen up the situation and enables the speaker to proceed in a

3

more relaxed, natural manner. When you are introduced to an individual, he shakes your hand and says how do you do. But when you are introduced to an audience, they just sit there—after some polite applause—and you become conscious of their anonymity and silence and even skepticism. If you can hear them laugh, you feel—perhaps irrationally—that they are with you, attentive and responsive.

Humor is of the greatest importance at the start of a speech because it puts the speaker personally and directly in communication with the audience. The religious evangelist warms to his subject as the congregation cries "Amen" or "Halleluja." The political orator, if he is skillful, uses staccato catch phrases and pauses that will cause him to be interrupted by applause, and the applause spurs him on. As for the ordinary speaker, the only reaction he can ever expect from the audience during the performance, to evidence appreciation or even attention, is laughter or at least a chuckle.

Another value of humor is that, even where the speech is read from a prepared text, the jokes are usually given extemporaneously. This gives the audience some chance to size up the personality of the speaker. He is then "being himself." If he can tell a joke with warmth and sparkle, he is probably a nice guy. If he can tell it cleverly and with no fumbles, he is probably a self-confident guy. If his humor seems spontaneous and has a genuine topical pertinence, he is probably an intelligent guy. If the humor is obviously original, based on some incident or remark the audience has just seen or heard, the speaker is an alert—perhaps even a brilliant—guy.

But the few moments at the beginning of a speech

when he is being humorous is usually the only time a speaker just talks to the audience, as he would to a group of friends around the lunch table. How often I have wished I could push aside the podium and microphones and visual aids and the other deterrents to naturalness and just talk in a conversational way to the audience. And I have often done it. Humor helps to put you in the mood to do it. Most of my hundreds of speeches to insurance and post office groups have been off the cuff and generously sprinkled with humor.

Another reason for using humor in a speech is that it is a sugar coating. You may decide to deviate from the norm and really say something in a speech rather than mouth a lot of platitudes. Even more important, you may decide to say something which you believe in and think is important to say even though it may be contrary to the thinking of your audience.

Controversy often
Inappropriate

I mention elsewhere various circumstances where it is inappropriate to make a controversial speech, such as at charity functions or at events where the speaker knows the program chairman expects him to avoid controversy.

There is the story about the town reprobate who was on his deathbed and a priest came in to administer the last rites.

"Andrew, I want you to renounce the devil," the priest said.

"I'm sorry, but I can't do it," the rounder replied. "At this point I'm in no position to offend anyone."

But there are many occasions where expressing views

5

which vary from those of the audience peps up a speaking appearance immeasurably. That is one reason for all the current interest in "panels" for speaking programs. It is the hope of stirring up a lively argument among the participants.

Humor Softens Controversy

A controversial speech which is delivered in a grim, severe, aggressive manner will only make the audience mad. On the other hand, if it is delivered in a good-humored vein, with a few laughs scattered through it, the audience is much more receptive, much more willing to ponder the new thoughts than to resent them.

Let us assume, for example, that a police chief is speaking before an audience of judges and he intends to tell them that he thinks judges generally are too lenient with criminals. If he starts right out in a hard-nosed fashion giving them that message, the reaction of the judges is likely to be:

"Who does this cop think he is, telling us about how to run our courts? What does he know about psychiatry, sociology, or jurisprudence?"

But let us assume the police chief starts out with this:

> A sharp character brought suit against a large store, claiming he had fallen on its slippery floor, injured his back, and become permanently and totally paralyzed from the waist down. The insurance lawyer, defending the suit, was sure the claimant was a faker and tried his best to prove it. But the jury brought in an award of $200,000.
>
> After the trial the lawyer walked over to the gloating plaintiff and said:

"You got your money. But you're never going to be able to enjoy it. I'm going to dog your steps until I prove you are a fake. Wherever you go, I'll be watching you. You'll never be able to get out of that wheel chair. You're not going to be any better off than if you really were paralyzed."

"Listen, chum," said the sharp one. "Now that we're being frank, I'll tell you something. Tomorrow the plushiest ambulance in town calls for me at my home and takes me to the airport. I get on a plane for Paris. In Paris another plush ambulance meets me, with a pretty French nurse. That ambulance drives me, oh so carefully, down to the Shrine at Lourdes in the south of France. And then you're going to see the greatest miracle take place that they have ever had!"

Creates Receptive Audience

This helps to put the audience in a more receptive mood. First, it gets them laughing. Second, it relates to their profession as lawyers. Third, assuming the police chief tells this urbane joke well, it tells the judges that he is no dummy.

Later in his speech he might introduce another story by saying that he isn't talking about minor offenders or people who may stray from the straight and narrow just one time.

During the early part of World War II some American troops were subjected to an intense, prolonged attack on Guadalcanal. When it was finally over, all hands had frayed nerves.

Three chaplains were with the troops, one priest, one Methodist minister, and one rabbi. When the attack was over, they decided to sneak away to a little shack in the jungle and play some poker in an effort to relax, even though they knew that the commanding colonel was violently opposed to gambling.

7

After they had been playing for half an hour or so, they heard someone coming through the trees. Sure enough, it was the colonel. Quickly they put the cards and the money under a box in the corner and when the colonel came in, they were all very innocently engaged in an animated chat.

"Have you been gambling in here?" the colonel thundered.

They all looked at him in surprise. He then looked the priest in the eye.

"Have *you* been gambling?"

The priest thought back about the terrible strain he had been under and how heroic he had been and deserving of a little respite. And he thought what this thing could do to his chance for a promotion in the Army and to his whole career as a member of the cloth. So under his breath he said a little prayer, asking forgiveness, and then he answered,

"Why, no, colonel. Not me."

The colonel turned on the Methodist.

"How about you?"

The Methodist had much the same thoughts as the priest—under strain, deserve some relaxation, damage to career, and in addition he thought: my priest friend here belongs to an older denomination than mine. He must know what he's doing. So the Methodist likewise said:

"No, colonel, absolutely not."

By then the colonel was really furious and, with red face, he glared at the rabbi.

"Then how about *you*?"

To which the rabbi opened his hands before him and said with a hurt voice:

"Who with?"

Humor Disarms Audience

In addition to using a light and friendly approach, our police chief will also disarm his audience by the technique of using some exaggerated examples which all the judges will agree with. He will thus identify himself with his hearers as being, like them, sound and reasonable.

For example, he will describe a case he "heard about" from one of his colleagues in an unnamed distant city where an "inexperienced and timid" judge gave a bank robber a suspended sentence, although it was his fourth offense!

The chief will then say:

> I am confident that the fine group of judges we have in this state are as appalled as I am with that sort of weak-kneed approach to law enforcement. I know our dedicated and highly trained judges do not want to see the civil liberties fanatics and bleeding hearts successful in their efforts to create an ever more impossible obstacle course for the police. I know that our judiciary believes that there must be a limit to the technicalities and the unrealistic theories that result in turning criminals loose to prey on innocent citizens.

The chief has followed through on his earlier softening up of the audience with humor, by "knowing" that these sound men agree with him on a number of things they, in fact, don't agree with.

The Sugar Pill

This approach to selling an audience might be called the sugar pill followed by the Trojan Horse. The jokes get them off their guard, and the follow-up puts the speaker inside their camp in a way that makes it difficult for them to extricate themselves.

So my third reason for using humor is that it can serve a far more important purpose than mere attention getting, or amusement. It can play a big part in making an audience willing to listen to and to think about new ideas. It makes it possible to give a speech that really says something and still doesn't rub the audience the wrong way. It helps to make the audience want to like the speaker and to want to agree with him or at least not to reject him out of hand.

During the 1964 presidential campaign, Dean Burch, the new Republican National Chairman, was scheduled to speak before the National Press Club in Washington. The audience was generally unsympathetic. But Burch made effective use of humor as a softening up technique. Whether he felt humorous himself—in that pessimistic atmosphere created by the polls—we can't know, but he had some amusing comments and he made the audience laugh. Here was an example of a man who is, by nature, somewhat grim and brittle, who was able to put himself over with some light remarks.

Personal Anecdotes

Anecdotes by the speaker about himself do not have to be screamingly funny in order to go over with an audience, provided they are told in an interesting, colorful way. Picturesque speech is itself one of the best forms of humor.

Here, for example, is the beginning of a speech by Dr. Max Rafferty, the elected State Superintendent of Public Instruction in California, delivered at Pepperdine College in Los Angeles. Rafferty is telling about his election campaign the previous November, in which he ran against Dr. Ralph Richardson:

> One gets all kinds of introductions in this business. Especially is this true in the hustle and bustle of a campaign

such as I was engaged in recently. Once I was introduced by a rather flustered lady as "Roctor Dax Mafferty!" An even more flustered gentleman struggled through a ponderous eulogy in the very, most bitter, heated phase of the campaign and finally wound up with a floral oratory in which he compared me with everybody from Daniel Webster on down, and then introduced me as "Dr. Ralph Richardson."

I'm reminded of the time I was in a motorcade at the midpoint of the campaign. I don't know whether any of you have ever been in a motorcade or not, but it's sort of the closest thing politics have to a football serpentine, homecoming night. Everybody gets in cars, decorates them with banners, sends balloons out the windows; boys proceed down the street trying to attract votes. And on this particular motorcade, they stuck me in the lead car and I felt pretty foolish, as you can imagine.

There we were tooting horns down through the middle of San Francisco. And to make things worse, on the side of the car, they had a larger than life picture of me—I take the world's worst picture—look like Dracula coming out of the swamp somewhere! This particular one was the one used throughout my campaign, and it had to be posed for 22 times before they could finally get one that even looked faintly human. Finally, they caught me absent-mindedly looking at the progress of a fly across the lens of the camera and they shot it quickly as my eyes were raised rather soulfully toward heaven with a sort of pious look, you know, and that's the one they used for lack of anything better.

Well, anyway, this was on the side of the car and the motorcade stopped at a San Francisco intersection, and there on the corner was a little old lady waiting for the red light to turn green so she could cross. Well, I'd always thought that all little old ladies lived in Pasadena, you know, but this one lived in San Francisco and she was a typical one. She had her hair in a bun behind her ears, and she had steel-rimmed glasses. She carried this little beaded string bag, and she was standing there waiting for the light to change. She saw the motorcade draw up. She looked at the picture on the side of the car, she took a step down from the curb, and she rapped with her handbag upon the glass window where I was sitting.

I carefully put down the window as quickly as possible (hoping to corral the elusive voice) and the lady said very primly and precisely, "I do not know your candidate, but my, he is good looking!" Well, I reacted just like Jack Benny. I said, "Well! thank you, madam." She took a step back up the curb, looked at me very severely over her steel-rimmed spectacles and she said, "Are *you* the candidate?" I said very proudly, "Yes, ma'am." She said, "Oh, no!"

II

_U_sing _H_umor in the

_B_ody of the _S_peech

There are two important reasons why
humor should be used in the body of
a speech as well as at the opening.

First is the "Surprise Symphony"
reason: to bring back the attention of
the audience by a change of pace.

I have read that the listening
span of the average person hearing a
speech is about two minutes. This may
be too cynical a figure. But any experienced speaker, no matter how skillful he is, will recall instances when
members of an audience have given
themselves away by some chance remark as having failed to listen.

Audiences Don't Listen

I once included in a half hour talk to a convention of Prudential insurance agents in Victoria, British Columbia, a ten-minute description of the Prudential's efforts to obtain authority to write a new type of insurance plan called the variable annuity. Later in the morning, one of the agents approached me with the obvious intention of showing interest in the company's problems.

"I was disappointed," he said, "that you didn't tell us anything this morning about the variable annuity."

Ouch!

I once listened to a speaker who got the pages of his text mixed up and read the same page twice. I couldn't observe that anyone in the audience noticed it.

I am positive that a completely meaningless series of stereotyped phrases could be inserted in most speeches and the audience would never know the difference.

Try This Simple Test

If you doubt this, try slipping this in, without a change of tone or expression, following some pages of generalized observations:

> In a time of crisis such as the present, with all the troubled world watching and the crushing weight of an uncertain future pressing down upon our overburdened shoulders, we must not fail to hesitate. We must not fall victim to those of little faith who refuse to sit idly by. Instead, we must march forward shoulder to shoulder with our departed forefathers, daring to grasp from their bold embrace the fruits of notable failure. I cannot stress this too strongly—even at the risk of seeming repetitious under the impact of alien ideology. We must have no false gods to deny it. The em-

14

phasis cannot be exaggerated. There are some, of course, who will agree. But with the help of loyal and intelligent people who are conscious of our true ideals they can be overcome. Conscientious devotion to consistency and reasonableness, in the face of problems that try men's souls, and despite overwhelming odds, will, with courage and dedication, be mercifully eliminated.

To understand why audiences do not really listen, one must understand why most audiences gather to hear speeches in the first place. As I mentioned in my introduction, speakers and speeches have become more numerous and more indispensable because of business expense tax rules, and restrictions imposed by company comptrollers. Many of the conventions and sales meetings and trade association gatherings are in fact held 1. because of the strong American urge to get together, talk shop, and socialize; 2. to reward the participants for an outstanding sales record; and 3. to give participants an expense paid or tax deductible excuse for a vacation away from home.

Surely no delegate departing for a convention of appliance dealers, chiropodists, the American Legion, or the Brotherhood of Locomotive Engineers would tell a friend he was going in order to hear the speeches. He would probably say instead that he was going in order to take in the World's Fair, play some golf, or spend a few days on the beach. Yet speeches there must be. Unless there is a serious program there might be trouble with the tax collector. And, even worse, the organization might not seem significant and worth belonging to.

There are other things that add to the obstacle course for speakers and speeches. Most of the speeches at big conventions and meetings will be from prepared texts. So the convention goer who does not attend or does not listen can always salve his conscience by telling himself he will read the speech later (he never does).

Topical Humor, a Sure Thing

The surest guarantee of success for humor is for it to have some clear connection with an incident that has just taken place at the particular gathering.

The most common way to do this is with a story or humorous comment related to something that has been said in a previous speech or introduction. Or it may relate to something about the location of the gathering or the menu or the service.

For example, a speaker might say, without warning, in the body of his speech:

> I noticed on the lobby bulletin board as I was coming in that another group is holding a convention in this hotel: the National Association of Morticians. [*True*] That's a very fine organization. Last year I made the principal address at the convention of that association in Cleveland. [*Not true*] It was on a topic of great importance to them. It took me weeks to prepare it. The title of my speech was "How to Look Sad at a $10,000 Funeral."

The audience feels a special appreciation and even participation in this kind of humor because many of them also saw the Morticians listed on the lobby bulletin board.

The people who can use this technique with special skill are those rare individuals who are quick enough to be able to make up humor to fit the occasion. President

Kennedy was superbly endowed with that ability. Sitting a few places away from him at a speakers' table, I have often observed his invariable practice of listening closely to the speakers preceding him and scribbling quick little notes on the back of his program or menu. Then when he stood up to speak his opening remarks would sparkle with wry, original, and highly pertinent witticisms tied in gracefully to remarks by others on the program.

This served him in particularly good stead at the big stag dinners given in Washington each year by the Alfalfa Club and the Gridiron Club. These are tough audiences, each made up of about 800 of the very top leaders in business, politics, and the press from all over the country. The Alfalfa Club has no purpose or function except to hold its annual prestige banquet at which someone is nominated to run for President on the Alfalfa Ticket. The Gridiron Club is an exclusive 50 member "club within a club" of the National Press Club. Its banquet features original skits and songs lampooning public figures. Here many a political truth is spoken in jest. The President, at each of these affairs, sits through several hours of talks and entertainment, often as the target, before he is called on for the final remarks. It is an ideal opportunity for weaving together various retorts on the evening's events. Kennedy was superb in that role.

III

Cautions on Use
of Humor

Note that in discussing the reasons why use of humor in a speech is important, I did *not* say it should be used to curry favor with the audience. To establish a connecting link and a rapport, yes. But to "butter up" the listeners, *no!*

Too often a speaker starts right off being apologetic for being on the program at all:

"My remarks will take only a few minutes."

"I won't bore you long with what I have to say."

"I know it is running late and

you are anxious to get out on the golf course so I will cut down my remarks."

"Any of you who may be interested in my subject can read the mimeographed text later at your convenience so I will just summarize some of the main points."

Don't Be Dull

One of the worst examples of this I ever observed was at an Annual Dinner of the Boy Scout leadership in Los Angeles. It was a big affair with a courteous, attentive crowd. The speaker was the Chancellor of the University of California at Los Angeles. He was a man of prestige and learning and the audience expected to hear something good.

He came to the podium with a weary, tired-of-it-all look, handled his prepared text in such a way that the audience became unavoidably conscious of it, and began as follows:

> I have read this speech to several other audiences before tonight. If there is anything that is more boring than hearing a speech for the fourth or fifth time it is *giving* it the fourth or fifth time.

He then proceeded to drone away from the text and demonstrated conclusively that he was indeed insufferably bored with the speech. It was too involved and complicated for that audience anyway and was a very poor performance.

Don't Be Apologetic

Very often speakers who feel apologetic about being before the audience at all will try to cater to the audience with excessive or inappropriate humor.

19

That may be all right for Las Vegas casino comedians but it is not all right for a normal speaking engagement.

One form of inappropriate humor is making fun in a cutting way of the introducer, the organization itself, the meal that has been served, others on the program, or the size or reactions of the crowd.

The Las Vegas comedian typically starts out like this:

> I wish all you people out there would shake your heads three times. No! Harder! Like this. Now, all together, one, two, three. *Well*. You *are* alive after all. I was beginning to wonder. Of course if rigor mortis *had* set in I wouldn't be too surprised after that meal we just ate. I've often wondered what happens to all those tired old TV dinners that nobody buys. It reminds me of the American who was telling his friend about going to dinner at an aristocratic country home in England: "If the soup had been as warm as the wine, and if the wine had been as old as the chicken, and if the chicken had been as plump as the waitress, and if the waitress had been as willing as the Duchess, it would have been one hell of an evening." Excuse me, sir, am I keeping you awake? Sorry, I'll talk more softly. I don't see the program chairman anywhere, and I don't blame him. He said this would be a live wire audience. Well someone seems to have blown a fuse. *Etc*.

Many speakers make the mistake of making fun of the arrangements. It is very bad form, for example, although frequently done in an effort to be funny, to read to the audience from a private memorandum furnished to speakers to show the time schedule.

> I have here a memorandum marked "confidential" which was given to me just before I came in by your dinner

> chairman, Mr. C. Mortimer Blatt. It says I was supposed to be called on at 8:23 and that I am supposed to sit down at 8:43. Well, that's a little difficult because it's already 9:51. And no wonder. Mr. Morley who introduced me was supposed to take just 1½ minutes to tell you how outstanding I am but of course it was impossible to even hit the high spots in that short time and he took 6¾ minutes.

The speaker should also not try to crack wise about the audience being smaller than he was promised.

And he should be extremely cautious about trying to be funny about the organization before which he is appearing. True, Franklin Roosevelt once opened a speech to the ultranationalistic Daughters of the American Revolution with the salutation "Fellow immigrants." But he was not seeking to endear himself to that immediate audience.

Avoid Bad Form

I have mentioned earlier that making fun of the introduction is very bad form. It is a mistake to call attention to errors and omissions made by the introducer. If the speaker is going to attempt some humorous observation about the introduction being too generous, he should be prepared with something good and should not blunder along with a graceless display of phoney modesty.

Here's an acknowledgement for an overflattering introduction:

> I appreciate that introduction. We all realize, of course, that introductions sometimes are too complimentary. It is like the man who saw a slightly familiar face in a crowded hotel lobby.

21

"Aren't you Smith who made a million dollars in oil in Oklahoma?" he asked.

The other man replied:

"Well, actually it wasn't Oklahoma, it was Oregon. And it wasn't oil, it was lumber. And it wasn't one million, it was two million. And I didn't make it, I lost it. And, by the way, my name is not Smith but Jones."

I remember one instance where an introducer blundered so incredibly that it was inevitable that the speaker would retaliate. After he had acquired round the world flight fame many years ago Wiley Post came to my home town of Springfield, Illinois, to visit Lincoln's Tomb and make a speech. Here's the way it went.

> INTRODUCER: Ladies and gentlemen, we are signally honored today by the presence of a world citizen who has deservedly been honored in many great cities for his historic accomplishments. It is a privilege to have such a famous man here to address us. I am proud to present . . . to present . . . uh, uh . . .

He *forgot* Post's name. Someone had to whisper it to him.

> POST: (*When he got to his feet*) Mr. Chairman, it is an honor to be in this world famous city. I have visited many of the famous capitals abroad but I have always looked forward to the opportunity of coming to this beautiful city of . . . uh, uh . . .

(Politicians, on whirlwind campaign trips, sometimes do make embarrassing mistakes about the name of the city they are visiting at the moment. In the 1936 campaign during a rear platform stop in Bloomington, Illinois, Roosevelt told the assembled townspeople how happy he was to be in "Bloomingburg.")

No Dirty Jokes

My most important caution on use of humor is: *don't use dirty jokes.*

Some consider it a cheap way to get a laugh from the audience. But it lowers the stature of the meeting and of the speaker. Most people, even though they may laugh at dirty jokes told in public speeches, lose respect for the speaker.

I believe strongly that the rule is no different for all male audiences than for mixed audiences. If someone is to get down in the gutter let it be some low-grade paid entertainer and not the speaker of the evening.

Deciding if a joke is inappropriate is easy. Use the same rule as the one for deciding whether a shirt is clean enough to wear to the office a second day: if you have doubts, *it isn't.*

This by no means excludes every joke that recognizes there are two sexes. Much delightful and sparkling humor has a bit of restrained spiciness.

Here's one in that category which fits nicely into a speech in which the speaker wants to express his thanks for being shown a good time at the convention where the speech is being given.

> A young man and a blonde came into a fashionable Fifth Avenue fur store on a Friday afternoon. The man told the clerk in a brusque manner that he wanted to look at the most expensive fur coat in the place. The clerk was a little doubtful and brought out a nice squirrel-skin job.
>
> "Take it away," said the customer impatiently. "Appar-

ently you didn't hear what I said. I want the *most expensive* coat you have."

Next the clerk tried a beaver coat, then a seal skin, and then a sheared raccoon, but each time with the same result. The man was getting very impatient. So finally the clerk shot the works and brought out a $5,000 mutation mink. When the man saw that, his eyes lit up. Turning to the blonde he said,

"That's the idea—finally. Try that on, honey. See how it looks."

It looked terrific.

The man looked it over critically while the blonde posed in front of the mirror.

"That's just what we want," said the man. "But the sleeves are a little short. Could you lengthen them and have it ready Monday?"

"Certainly, sir, certainly. Anything you say." The clerk was now fawning.

"And when I come in to pick this up I'll want to charge it. Here's my card. Get all your credit checking done before I get here. I'm too busy to be held up with details."

There was much bowing and scraping as the couple swept out of the store.

Monday morning the man arrived at the store alone. The minute he walked in the clerk rushed up to him shaking his fist, followed by the floor walker, the chief buyer, the manager, and the credit manager. All were shouting at him angrily.

"We've looked you up," the credit manager barked, "and you have no more credit than a mouse. You couldn't charge a toothbrush."

"Now calm yourself," said the man, "I haven't taken anything out of your store. . . . I just came in to thank you for a wonderful weekend."

Frequently someone at the speakers' table is called on "to say just a few words."

Here is a cute story with a very mild sex angle that is highly appropriate for starting some brief, impromptu remarks.

> A young soldier and his girl friend hurried into a country judge's office late on a Friday afternoon and asked him to marry them.
>
> "Got a license?" he asked.
>
> "No, judge," said the would-be bride. "John here just got home for a weekend leave and the clerk's office is already closed."
>
> "Sorry," said the judge. "No license, no marriage."
>
> "But, judge," pleaded the girl. "John is just here for these two days. He has to be back at camp first thing Monday morning."
>
> "Can't help you," snapped the judge. "Rules is rules."
>
> "But, judge," said the girl, "couldn't you say just a few words to tide us over the weekend?"

Needless to say don't use "bathroom" humor. People who are obsessed with that type of story—and there are quite a few such people—must have some unpleasant psychopathic disturbance.

Some years ago, there was actually a book dealing entirely with toilets, which people I had previously thought to have normal good taste sent around as Christmas presents.

And, of course, Chick Sale humor was considered a real side splitter in its day. But that day is long since gone. People get around more now and the crude type of rustic humor has seen its day.

Bathroom jokes are not only unfunny—they are unsophisticated.

Beware of Spoofs

Another type of speech material which requires great care and caution is something which sounds true but which only the most alert and sophisticated members of the audience will recognize as a spoof.

At the Republican National Convention at San Francisco in 1964, U.S. Senator Peter Dominick of Colorado went overboard with a spoof. The convention was debating a proposed amendment to the platform expressing disapproval of "extremism." In opposing the amendment, Dominick wanted to make the point that some of our early American patriots were considered extremists by their contemporaries.

With a straight face and no advance explanation, Dominick read to the convention and television audience an "editorial from the *New York Times* in 1765" attacking Patrick Henry for being an "extremist."

There wasn't any *New York Times* in 1765 but rank and file members of the party couldn't be expected to know that. The whole thing was supposed to be a "joke." However, it caused not laughs but confusion and criticism and required Dominick to issue an explanation.

When humor requires a public explanation it means it wasn't humor in the first place, or at least that it was used before the wrong audience.

One of the reasons for this is that many people in audiences listen uncritically. They aren't sitting there saying about every thought and sentence: "Is that accurate on the basis of what I know?" If the speaker inadvertently says "millions" instead of "billions" in giving the amount of the Federal budget or the national debt, very few listeners will notice.

Then, too, many people just aren't alert to miscellaneous things in their surroundings.

A particular scenic cave in western Virginia carefully places bumper stickers on the cars of all its visitors and these stickers abound in the area within 100 miles, in every direction, of the cave. In a speech during the 1964 presidential campaign I told the audience I didn't put much faith in the Gallup Poll or the Harris Poll; that the only one I relied on was my own private "bumper sticker poll" which I took myself; that it showed to me conclusively that the one who was going to win was a man I didn't even know but he obviously was more popular than any other candidate: a fellow named LURAY CAVERNS!

I should have saved myself the trouble. It didn't go over.

I should have recalled that when a prominent man, in introducing me to make a speech, used another man's biography, no one in the audience seemed to notice.

Debunkers Make Enemies

Another form of humor that is ticklish is debunking national heroes and revered parts of history.

It may be funny in California to say there never would have been a Texas if there had been a back door in the Alamo. But it isn't funny in Houston or Fort Worth.

It may be amusing before a group of History Ph.D's to point out that George Washington had a bad temper or that Lincoln told some rough jokes. But it isn't good for a D.A.R. convention.

Not long ago a speaker started out his talk to a

group of businessmen by stating that the Pilgrim Fathers attempted, when they arrived in 1620, to set up a communistic economic system. I doubt if it was a good idea to get all those childhood images of the Mayflower group associated with Lenin and Stalin.

National Idols

The following, on the need for national idols, was used in a speech by Charles H. Brower, advertising executive. He entitled it: "The Return of the Square."

> We refer to our humor as sick, sick, sick, and it is, is, is. Mother used to get cards on Mother's Day, expressing in some way the fact that she was loved and wanted. Now if she is lucky she gets a card that shows Whistler's mother flat on her back and a caption that says, "You're not the only one who's off her rocker." Otherwise she may get a card that says, "Want to lose 15 ugly pounds? . . . Then cut off your head."
>
> Mort Sahl, to me, represents the cackling of despair. And even Bob Newhart, clean and crew-cut, and buttoned-down as he is, cannot resist the temptation to give a hot foot now and then to our national idols.
>
> I claim we need those idols. And I am not going to be amused by a skit in which Lincoln's publicity man tells him to "write it on envelopes, Abe" or "Why don't you take it easy tonight, Abe, and take in a show?"
>
> Laughter today is stored in Hollywood in cans, just as the gold was once stored at Fort Knox. It is taken out as needed and pasted onto TV films. And the laugh track tips us off to when things are funny.
>
> But I want to laugh when I am amused. And I want to decide what I think is funny. And this, I suppose, will mark me as a square. And if it does, I will be in pretty good company. For this country was discovered, put together, fought for and saved by squares. It is easy to prove that

Nathan Hale, Patrick Henry, Paul Revere, George Washington, Benjamin Franklin, and almost anyone else you care to include among our national heroes were squares—by simply thinking what they might have said had they not been squares.

NATHAN HALE: Me spy on those British! Are you trying to be funny? Do you know what they do with spies they catch? I'll give you a newsflash, chum. They *hang* them.

PAUL REVERE. What do you mean—me ride through every Middlesex village and town? And in the middle of the night yet. Why pick on me? Am I the only man in Boston with a horse?

PATRICK HENRY: Sure, I'm for liberty. First, last and always. But we've got to be a little realistic. We're a pretty small outfit. If we start pushing the British around someone is going to get hurt.

GEORGE WASHINGTON: Gentlemen, I am honored. But I do wish you would try someone else. Let's say General Gates. I'm just getting things organized at Mount Vernon. Also you might say I had already served my time. Against the French you know.

BENJAMIN FRANKLIN: What we really need as Ambassador to France is a young man. I'm 70 years old. It's time a new generation took over.

Here, then, is a check list of cautions on use of humor.

1. Don't apologize for being on the program.
2. Don't ridicule the organization or the occasion.
3. Don't make fun of the arrangements.
4. Don't use dirty jokes or bathroom tales.
5. Don't use a spoof that the audience won't grasp.
6. Don't make fun of national heroes and the national heritage.

IV

$\mathcal{P}$lanning the $\mathcal{P}$rogram

The success of a speaking event begins with the people in charge of the advance planning: the program chairman, the dinner chairman, the publicity chairman, and the head of the organization.

At the very outset they should agree on the following:

1. If the event is worth doing it is worth doing right.
2. The event should be a pleasant experience—not drudgery for the participants and the audience.
3. Someone with experience and know-how should be put in charge.

This means that a dinner chairman or program chairman should not attempt to run the show unless he really knows how. He should not extemporize or attempt to get by on guesswork or instinct.

Secure Professional Aid

If the organization has money to hire a capable professional it should do so. If it is a trade association with a full-time, paid executive secretary, it should insist that he make himself an expert on putting on effective programs. If there is no money and no staff, a program manager with experience in planning and following through should be recruited.

Let us assume we are preparing for a large public dinner to launch a capital fund drive for the new Community Hospital. I choose this example because it is a "first time" event without the set pattern of the standard annual dinners of various civic and charitable organizations.

The first thing to do is to figure out how it can be made into a prestige event which will be worth the time of a speaker who will be a drawing card. A good speaker is much more likely to accept if the event is to be held in the best hotel ballroom in town rather than in the YMCA basement. He may even be more inclined to accept if the affair is "black tie," indicating that the committee and the audience consider it a "Special" evening.

Choose Date with Care

The date is important. Be sure there is no competitive event of the same general character on the same night or even during the same week. The Chamber of

Commerce usually keeps a master schedule. A fund raising dinner for a hospital could be a huge flop if it came two nights after a fund raising dinner for the local college.

If feasible set a theme for the evening. Don't just rely on "We need money. Come across." Instead plan to explain to the prospects with visual aids, brochures, and publicity the extra costs of new medical techniques and equipment such as open heart surgery or iron lungs.

Make a realistic estimate of how many guests you can expect. Think out and decide in advance answers to the questions an experienced speaker may ask when he is invited. For example, decide on the total elapsed time from beginning to adjournment. How many speakers will there be? Will there be several featured speakers or one main speaker? Is there an original or nearly original gimmick that can make the meeting different and productive? For example, how about having the dinner on a boat, or even on a round trip special train to a nearby city?

Have One Boss

One of the worst hazards for a successful luncheon or dinner meeting is "too many bosses." With all due respect, it has been my experience that this is most frequently true when ladies are in charge.

One lady may have arranged with the banquet manager that the microphone will not be turned on until after dessert is served. Then during the meal another committee member, noting that the program is running behind schedule, rushes up to the toastmaster and tells him to introduce the head table after the main course and before the dessert is served. In the meantime, despite a crowded schedule, another committee member may insist that the Chairman of the County Board, who has accepted at the last minute, should be called on for a few words. Likely as not such an added starter is running for reelection in a hot campaign and supporters of his opponent will be irked by his unscheduled appearance.

One of my most chaotic public appearances resulted from serving as volunteer auctioneer at a ladies charity function in Washington. The donated items ranged from a buffalo skin coat to a cigarette holder that had been given by President Franklin Roosevelt to Chief Justice Fred Vinson. A previously mild-mannered congressional wife suddenly turned into one of the Furies as she stood behind me, bossing and criticizing, during my auctioneering efforts. I never once said "going, going, gone" but she whispered loudly that I had shut off the bidding too soon. Yet when the bidding dragged she was impatient for me to go on to the next item. Another lady complained I was offering the items in the wrong order, although still another was handing them up to me.

Advance planning as to who will be boss and of what is essential for a successful meeting.

Get a Good M.C.

There should also be careful thought as to who will be master of ceremonies. Many a dinner becomes committed to a dull and drab performance because the chairman of the organization or the dinner chairman is automatically selected for M.C. even though he has a disastrous lack of personality for the assignment.

The M.C. should be chosen with the same care as the speaker. The qualifications:

1. Wit and sparkle.
2. Tact and discretion so that he will avoid, for example, "taking over" and upstaging the speaker.
3. Brevity.
4. Punctuality.
5. Popularity in the community.

Contrary to common belief, the M.C. does not need to have had any previous connection or acquaintance with the organization putting on the dinner. The most high powered fund raising drives are the Israel Bond dinners. Usually a prominent public official is recruited as speaker. But the M.C.'s role is recognized as being most important. He may be a well-known man from the entertainment world.

In any event there is much to do in planning a speaking event before the speaker is chosen and invited.

V

Choosing the Speaker

In choosing a speaker it is important to pick someone who is well known rather than an unknown—no matter how skillful or entertaining the unknown may be.

Naturally, the ideal is a well-known and effective speaker. But assuming such a paragon isn't to be had, the president of the state university, located 100 miles away, is a better choice, even though he is a dull speaker, than the new assistant professor of biology at the local junior college, who is thoroughly amusing before an audience.

To understand why this is true

we need to analyze what most program chairmen are trying to achieve through the selection of the speaker.

Speaker Must Draw Crowd

First, they want to draw a crowd. There is status symbol value in going to hear a well-known speaker. There is conversation value in telling friends that one has seen and heard a well-known man "in person." If prospective attenders of the meeting think that it is going to be a popular event which will draw a big crowd they will *not* stay away to avoid the congestion. They will make a special effort to be on hand so they won't miss something and won't feel left out when their friends talk about having been present. It is the same way with a restaurant. If it has the reputation of being popular and crowded, with a wait required before being seated, people will flock to the place. On the other hand, if there are always plenty of empty tables, no matter how good it is the customers will think it is not the place to be and will wish they had gone someplace else.

I have always thought that if I owned a roadside restaurant I would buy about 20 cheap but presentable used cars and park them in front. Then people driving by would think they would find a crowd inside and would stop. People hate to go to restaurants or theaters or speaking events where there are lots of empty seats. It makes them feel they had poor judgment in deciding to come.

A program chairman is, in a very real sense, "putting on a show." He may feel certain that he has "discovered" a terrific new star on the knife and fork circuit.

But if the prospective audience has never heard of this new find our program chairman will be in the same unhappy situation as a night club proprietor who gives top billing to an unknown performer. People won't come.

Program Can Increase Prestige

The second thing the program chairman is trying to do is to add prestige to the meeting or the organization. It may be easy to get an acceptance from the local police judge or from the assistant superintendent of the Methodist District, but it doesn't add much to the standing or position of the group that is having the meeting. It would be a real coup for the state garden club to get the Secretary of the Interior to be the principal speaker at the annual meeting, regardless of whether the particular incumbent happened to be a good speaker. He would be a far better choice than the head of the section on botany at the Library of Congress even if that person were in fact a Bob Hope who had been hiding his light under a bushel.

One might ask: Isn't it a prime motive of the program chairman to try to make people in the audience glad they came?

My answer is that that is something the program chairman should hope for. But he cannot afford to make it the controlling consideration. If he doesn't draw a crowd, those who do come are unlikely to be glad they came even if the speaker is good.

As I have said, if the program chairman can choose and obtain an acceptance from a speaker who has both name and ability, that is much to be desired. But since the two qualities do not automatically or even predominantly come together, name is more important.

Speaker Must Suit Audience

Program chairmen often overlook the fact that an important title will not invariably assure a crowd *unless* the title indicates a field of interest and speech content which will appeal to the prospective audience. The head of the Fedreal Bureau of Roads has a big title and an enormous responsibility. However, it is doubtful if he would draw a crowd to a meeting of the state retail druggists association. They are far more likely to be interested in hearing from the head of the Food and Drug Administration, the Chairman of the Federal Trade Commission, or a prominent member of Congress who has been active in an investigation of the drug industry.

I was subjected to one of my most uncomfortable nights because a prominent lady refused to believe me when I told her that as Postmaster General I could not draw a crowd to her big evening meeting. It was a fund raising affair in Detroit for the Seven Eastern Women's Colleges (Vassar, Smith, etc.). It was to be held in the new 4,000 seat auditorium downtown on the lakefront. There was to be nothing on the program but the speech —no music, no name M.C., no food, no cocktails, nothing. Only a handful of public figures in the whole country could be expected to draw 4,000 listeners on a weekday evening in Detroit under those difficult circumstances.

The prominent lady, however, had heard me speak at a bar association dinner. Because she liked my speaking style and observed that I could talk about things other than the Post Office, she mistakenly assumed that *everyone else* would know I was a versatile speaker and that I would not be confined to remarks about postal rates, third class circular mail, or the Post Office budget. How wrong she was!

I tried my best to decline but I was obligated to the distinguished lady and she had asked me so long in advance I couldn't very well say I had a previous commitment. A prospective speaker is the best judge of his own drawing power. I was frank and realistic about what kind of crowd I could attract, but, unfortunately, I allowed myself to be pressured into accepting. After all, it was for a "good cause" and I was told that I was just being too modest.

As the fatal night approached I received a strong advance warning that the tickets weren't going well. An aggressive lady, whom I shall call Mrs. X, and whom I had never met or seen or heard of, turned out to be the one really in charge. As so often happens my distinguished friend had disappeared from all connection with the actual running of the gathering. She had merely been the bait. Now I was in the hands of strangers and being treated like a hired hand.

Mrs. X telephoned long distance to suggest—or rather to announce—that she was going to promote the $5 a head gathering among the 20,000 employees of the Detroit Post Office. She "knew" they would want to come because of their "big boss" being in town, etc. She overlooked the fact that I had been through that routine many times before and had a strong policy against it. I did not believe in shaking down loyal postal employees, just because of their loyalty to the head of the Postal

Service, to make them ante up money for a cause of no interest to them. It was particularly difficult for me to see why rank and file postal employees, half of them colored, and none of them rich, would want to contribute money to Vassar, Wellesley, Radcliffe, etc. These particular schools are not exactly pockets of poverty, and postal employees had plenty of chances to see me without charge since I traveled a great deal and always visited the work room floor of the local post office when I came to a city for any purpose.

I told Mrs. X politely but firmly that postal employees were not to be invited or contacted or involved in any way. I could see she was not going to take no for an answer.

A week before the gathering she called again and was even more insistent about the need for drawing a crowd from the postal employees. Just as insistently I said absolutely not.

When I arrived in Detroit I soon found that Mrs. X had ignored my instructions and had created a situation difficult for all concerned by inviting post office people. Her rather posh group of Eastern college alumnae was having a pre-speech reception and dinner for 100 people or so at the leading private club in town and had invited the heads of the local branches of the postal unions. These gentlemen, many of them colored, were definitely uncomfortable in these fancy surroundings. When I arrived I found them huddled together off in one corner. Instead of being able to fraternize with my hosts and other guests from the Detroit community, I hustled over to make the postal leaders comfortable. They promptly blossomed, produced a photographer for group pictures and much handshaking. All in all it was a most inappropriate and incongruous situation—just exactly what I had tried to prevent.

There were only 700 people in the 4,000 seat auditorium.

Mrs. X blamed it all on the local newspaper strike which had been going on for weeks, and which, according to her, prevented the publicity which would have drawn a crowd. There was no use arguing that point with her. However, it is perfectly clear that people do not come to fund raising affairs for causes to which they are not committed merely because they read advance publicity in a newspaper. They might come if the speaker were to be Billy Graham or Adlai Stevenson or John Glenn. But they won't come on their own initiative to hear a speaker of limited renown unless someone does a selling job on them. The organization putting on the affair must stir up a crowd. One of the standard ways is by giving dinner parties at private homes in advance of the speech event. Most ladies invited to provide a come-on for the speaker by giving such parties at their homes will not be so calculating as to conclude that it would be cheaper to buy 20 tickets outright than to put on a dinner for 20 ticket purchasers.

A speaker can help to draw a crowd, as I discuss later, by a catchy title. If I had not had scruples against ballyhooing such an ugly subject, I could have talked about pornography in the mails and titled my remarks as "Sex Traffic in the Mails" or "Protecting Our Youth from the Smut Peddlers."

One of my predecessors made a career out of making speeches on dirty books and dirty pictures. In contrast I felt that the problem called for a tougher enforcement crackdown rather than speechmaking.

Specialties May Be of Topical Interest

A person whose specialty might not ordinarily stir much interest can succeed in drawing a crowd if he is connected with a problem of widespread interest. The head of the United States Public Health Service might normally not be much of a drawing card at a convention of advertising men. However, he might become a major attraction as a result of issuing a report on the hazards of cigarette smoking. The head of the city water department might suddenly acquire appeal as a speaker before the chamber of commerce annual dinner if the city were threatened with a serious water shortage.

In choosing speakers from government it is important to bear in mind that certain agencies have, in the public mind, far more glamour than others. Foreign policy, defense, the FBI, and space projects are far more appealing to general audiences than the Department of Commerce, the Customs Bureau, or the Post Office.

As a rule a government official with an important sounding title in the foreign policy field is a good bet as a speaking attraction. The newspapers do a pretty good job of creating the impression that we are on the brink of war a good part of the time. There is always at least one foreign policy crisis around and sometimes two or three. Keeping informed about foreign affairs is considered far more fashionable than knowing about proposals for revising the federal budget or about federal aid to highway construction.

42

Typical Audience
Conservative

Another rule of thumb is that most service clubs, trade associations, women's clubs, and the like are conservative politically. Whatever the strength of the liberals or spenders as shown at the most recent election, the groups I mention prefer conservative speakers who offer catchword solutions to public problems.

With the exception of audiences drawn from labor unions, teachers, or northern Democratic party workers, most people who come to hear speakers are from the conservative stratum of society and many are suburbanites. They are likely to prefer a speaker who tells them the government is too big, taxes are too high, government spending is out of control, and we are not tough enough in our foreign policy. They do not want to hear a speaker who tells them that there are many pressing public problems to which there is no easy solution, that times have changed, that we must adjust, etc. They prefer a speaker who agrees with what they have been saying to each other at their luncheon clubs and card parties, and with what they have been reading in the *Reader's Digest* or on the editorial page of the conservative local newspaper.

Don't Aim Too High

In this important area of choosing a speaker, there is the problem best described as "aiming too high." There is no point in inviting the President of the United States to speak at a routine weekly meeting of a small town Kiwanis Club. There is no point in asking Bob Hope to speak at the Kickoff Dinner of the Oshkosh Community Chest Drive.

43

The program committee needs to be realistic. If one and then another person, who is too busy and too important, is asked to speak at an event which he will clearly consider not worth his while, much time will be lost and it may be necessary, in last minute desperation, to take just anyone.

(In the next chapter I cover another aspect of this "aiming too high" problem, i.e., how to make the event seem worthwhile to a very important person.)

Everything else being equal (which is seldom the case), there are some additional points to watch for in choosing a speaker. Since the "ideal" speaker is seldom available it may be necessary to select someone who lacks one or more of the desirable features.

Avoid Egotist

It is well to avoid a speaker who will "talk down" to the audience. A sophisticated novelist talking to a state woman's club convention might well regard them as a collection of Helen Hokinson types and treat them accordingly. No matter how prestigious, a speaker who is egotistical and shows it is not likely to go over well. Authors particularly are inclined to be a cocky set.

There is the story of the conceited author who had been talking at length to a lady at a cocktail party. Finally he said condescendingly:

"We've talked about me long enough. Let's talk about you. What do *you* think of my new book?"

Another danger is a speaker who will talk over the heads of his audience. He may be too technical, too complicated or he may go into too much detail about things the audience is not that interested in.

He may be like the father of the little boy who asked his mother what a ballistic missile was. She said, "Why don't you ask your father?"

The boy answered: "I don't want to know that much about it."

It may be all well and good to have a speaker talk on "Free Trade" to a Lions Club Convention but not if he is going to cover all the technical fine points about non-tariff barriers to trade, antidumping laws, countervailing duties and the like.

There is another story of a young boy who asked his mother, "Where did I come from?"

She was taken aback because of his youth but decided to make the big plunge and with considerable embarrassment gave him the fundamentals about sex and child-birth. He listened with interest. When she was through she inquired: "Why do you ask?"

"Oh," he said. "Bobby down the street said he came from Pittsburgh."

Avoid Stale Speaker

Another type of speaker to avoid is one who has become "old stuff" to the particular audience. The state banking commissioner who has been in office for some time and usually gives about the same old speech will not be a drawing card at a bankers' convention. The female member of the city council may have appeared so often before local women's groups that they will feel they have heard everything she has to say.

Then there is the problem of whether the speaker will be subject to reasonable control. Will he stay at least somewhat within the theme and the time limit? Will he avoid being too controversial for the particular audience and occasion? Is he unreliable? Have there been instances where he did not show up for a speech on time or even at all?

It is better to choose someone that one of the members of the program committee has actually heard. This will help to avoid getting saddled with someone who tells overly suggestive jokes, talks too long, or has other serious drawbacks.

VI

Sources of Speakers

Too often a group sitting down to choose a speaker has no source material other than the casual knowledge of those present. As a result the choice usually falls on one whom someone in the group has heard recently.

"We had Dr. Tompkins of the State Museum at Rotary a few weeks ago and he was real good."

But Dr. Tompkins talked about a pack trip in the Canadian Wilderness and the program being planned relates to raising capital funds for a new old people's home.

It is important to broaden the

47

base of suggestions and possibilities for just the right speaker.

Here are some sources of ideas or names:

1. Program chairmen of other somewhat similar organizations.
2. The executive secretary of the local chamber of commerce.
3. The president or public relations vice president of a university or college.

If an honorarium is available then a professional lecture bureau can be consulted. Some excellent speakers make the rounds under the auspices of these bureaus and they have experience in deciding what speaker will fit a particular audience.

Corporate Officers

Some large corporations have officers or "consultants" who travel about almost constantly making speeches before assorted audiences. Some of these, such as Kenneth McFarland, who claims some kind of connection with General Motors, mix jokes and reactionary political observations into a potpourri which goes over big with most audiences. He does not include any plugs for General Motors or the automobile industry.

James DuPont of the DuPont Corporation was a nervous, uneasy speaker when I heard him but the large dinner audience of real estate men and their ladies liked his modesty and his down-to-earth material. Also, no doubt, they were impressed by hearing a real, live, breathing member of the great DuPont family.

Some corporate presidents, for one reason or another, make themselves very available to travel around and make speeches. It may or may not be popular with their boards of directors, but if the company has a prominent name they make a good source of speakers.

Other corporate executives sometimes have impressive titles but practically no duties other than going around and creating good public relations by making speeches. James Aloysius Farley, my famous predecessor as Postmaster General, is President of Coca-Cola International. He attends 100 banquets a year. Of course, he does not speak at all of them but he makes many speeches all over the country, usually on patriotic themes.

Consult "Vital Speeches"

There are various ways of ascertaining who is available on the speechmaking circuit. One is to consult recent issues of the monthly magazine *Vital Speeches* which you can find in the Public Library.

One useful "source" of speakers is the expert: decide on a topic which will be of current interest to the audience and then consult experts as to who would be qualified to discuss that topic. The head of the Astronomy Department at the State University would not always be a drawing card. But his rating would go way up if he were talking about the Ranger moon photos soon after the Ranger project was achieved.

Town Hall in Los Angeles, on whose Board of Governors I served when I lived there, is an organization principally devoted to arranging weekly luncheon speaking programs for male audiences. The Commonwealth

Club in San Francisco and the Commercial Club in Chicago are similar.

Political Speakers

Town Hall has a continuing and challenging job of getting a name speaker every week without paying an honorarium or even travel expenses. One thing they do is to maintain liaison with the Los Angeles headquarters of the two political parties so as to obtain advance notice of visits by prominent political figures. If a well-known office holder such as Wayne Morse or Thruston Morton is going to be in town for a committee meeting on urban renewal, he may very well be willing and even eager to make use of Town Hall's podium for a speech.

Town Hall also broadens its base for suggestions by having its executive director pay visits to its friends in Washington, such as myself and Senator Tom Kuchel, to pick up ideas about prospective speakers. In this way it obtains leads not only as to which government officials are good speakers, but also as to when they will be in California.

In most of the larger cities there are one or more organizations which do this kind of conscientious job in preparing an inventory of eligible speakers and following their schedules. In some cases they may know of suitable speakers who do not quite fit their requirements but whose names they would be glad to pass along to an inquiring program chairman.

Most of the better speakers are busy people and even if the approach to them is skillful they will not be

able to accept. Therefore, the effective program committee should have a second, third, and fourth choice decided
on, rather than giving in to a flurry of desperate regroup-
ing in the event the first choice declines.

VII

ℐnviting the 𝒮peaker

This is the most important part of all.

Most of the sought-after speakers will be extremely busy men. The really prominent ones may be receiving several or even dozens of speaking invitations every week.

The important thing is to overcome their natural inclination to decline by convincing them that the event is going to be valuable, enjoyable, or both, to the particular speaker.

Too often an organization does all the right things in planning the meeting, choosing the speaker, arranging the advance publicity, and all the rest. And then everything goes down the drain because of the awkward way in which the speaker is invited.

Personal Invitation Best

There is one specific best way to increase the chances for an acceptance to a speaking invitation: have the prospect contacted in person by someone he knows and trusts, as is done in this phone call:

> Hello, Ralph. This is Fred Fairfax calling from Omaha. How's everything going? We missed you at the twenty-fifth reunion last June. Ralph, I know you're busy but I think this is something that is really worthwhile for your department (company, state, foundation, etc.). The Omaha Foreign Affairs Council is having their big annual dinner on October 24, United Nations Day. Last year they had as their main speaker Senator Bill Fulbright. The year before that they had Averill Harriman. They have an audience of about 900 of the top business and civic leaders in eastern Nebraska. This year the program committee considered some 25 names and agreed unanimously that they wanted you. They knew you and I were close friends and since I'm an active member of the Council I agreed to call you.

In this telephone conversation Fred Fairfax has accomplished several important things:

1. He has approached Ralph as an old friend whose judgment on the importance of the event Ralph can trust.
2. He has associated Ralph with high prestige figures who have spoken to the group in previous years.
3. He has promised a good audience—not merely large (that is 90 per cent of it), but also made up of important people.

As a result an atmosphere has been created which makes it difficult for Ralph to refuse—unless he has a firm previous commitment.

Chances are that Ralph will consult his calendar and give his old friend Fred an answer right then and there. If he says he has a previous commitment, the Omaha Foreign Affairs Council has at least avoided that most difficult problem—a long-delayed answer, which cuts down the time for inviting someone else.

If Ralph is an old hand, with enough mileage on him to make him skeptical even of a call by "old friend" Fred, he will decline to commit himself during the telephone call but will ask Fred to send him a letter giving all the details about the event. This has several advantages from Ralph's point of view. It gives him time to assess the priorities. And it tends to pin down somewhat such often exaggerated facts as promised size of audience. While awaiting the letter, Ralph, assuming he really is a busy man much in demand as a speaker, may check with the offices of Senator Fulbright and Ambassador Harriman to discover whether they were satisfied with their appearances before the group.

It would have improved the chances for an affirmative answer even more if Fred and one or two others from the Omaha Council could have called on Ralph and invited him face to face.

Don't Extend Invitation through Paid Staff Member

The very worst way to extend an invitation is for a paid staff member of an organization, who does not know the invitee at all, to write him a letter over his own signature. The staff member may feel sure that his letter describing the fine standing of the group will do the trick. But he overlooks the fact that it is highly unlikely "Ralph" actually wants to go to Omaha to make a speech even under ideal circumstances. And a letter from a stranger, no matter how persuasively phrased, is easy to decline.

If the invitee is a federal appointive official the chances of a favorable response are greatly improved by having the invitation extended through a member of Congress. For appointive officials it is desirable, if feasible, to first sell the top political official of the department who will then be sure to give his approval if the subordinate checks with him before accepting.

If a personal visit or a telephone call is not feasible it is doubly important that the telegram or letter extending the invitation come from someone who has a personal acquaintance with the invitee.

Frequently, if the person attempting to call the invitee by long distance is unable to get through to him because he is in a meeting or out of town, the person calling will give the substance of the invitation to the invitee's secretary to be passed on to her boss. This is poor policy. It isn't possible to relay enough detail to do a proper selling job. And the secretary may think the boss has been wearing himself out on speechmaking trips anyway and may damn the whole idea with faint praise.

Make Offer Attractive

In addition to making the speechmaking session itself sound worthwhile, the group extending the invitation can arrange other collateral events which will increase the chance for an acceptance.

For example: The Chamber of Commerce of Billings, Montana, may be trying to get as the speaker for their annual dinner a very prominent Easterner who lived in Billings a few years as a youth and went to high school there. Even though the man has not been back to Billings for many years he will hardly be attracted to this distant and rather hard to get to place just by an invitation to make a speech. But before inviting him the Chamber lines up a group of his old high school friends, still in Billings, who will be glad to give a luncheon for him. And they find they can arrange for him to lay the cornerstone for the new addition to the high school he attended. As a result, when they telephone him, they have an appealing and flattering package to offer him.

In another case the locality may have an especially fine golf course and the invitee, who loves golf, may be tempted by an offer to arrange a game for him there during his visit. I can even imagine a place in the West getting an acceptance from Defense Secretary Bob McNamara by promising him a mountain to climb.

But the speaking event must not be made to seem an unimportant incidental. It must be built up as much as is fairly justified. The invitee will be interested in knowing about probable publicity of the speech. If he is a businessman he may want to know what potential sources of business may be represented in the audience.

VIII

ℒeveling with the ℐpeaker

A speaker can make a really good speech only if he is in a good mood.

For this reason it is absolutely vital to see that nothing happens before he starts to talk which will cause him to be preoccupied or irritated.

The most common source of irritation is wide disparity between what the speaker was told when he was invited and what is in fact the situation when he arrives to make the speech.

Don't Exaggerate

It is a great temptation—which few program chairmen can resist—to give the sought-for speaker highly unrealistic and exaggerated promises as to the number who will be in the audience, the important personages who will attend, the publicity which will be obtained, and the relationship of the speech to the total program.

The invitation may say that the person being asked will be making the "featured" or the "keynote" speech, that there will be "at least" 1,000 people in the audience, that the Mayor and the Governor will be at the speakers' table, and that there will be extensive publicity, both in advance and after the speech.

When the speaker arrives at the place where the speech is to be given—and it is too late for him to change his mind—he will likely as not be told something like this by a harried and apologetic program chairman:

> We're still hoping for a satisfactory turnout tonight. We have 300 reservations and have set up 50 extra places just in case. Unfortunately we didn't realize until we became committed to this particular date that this is the night of the Chamber of Commerce annual dinner and a lot of people who would ordinarily be at our affair feel obligated to go to that. The Governor and the Mayor will be at the Chamber of Commerce but the State Auditor has promised us faithfully that he will drop in at our pre-dinner reception if he possibly can. We had hoped one of the newspapers would send somebody over but this is the week of the American Legion Convention here and the reporters are spread too thin. We're particularly sorry because after we talked to you it turned out our National President was going to be able to be here and we wanted a big crowd for his keynote speech which is the next thing on the program after you. Incidentally, I imagine it won't be any problem for you to cut down your remarks to 12 or 15 minutes. We don't want to run too late.

Send Speaker Memorandum

It is only fair to be forthright at the time of inviting a speaker and to give him a memorandum about what he can expect.

Here is a sample of such a memorandum outlining the information which the speaker should be given in advance.

EVENT: Annual Dinner of the Boston Chapter of the American Red Cross.

PLACE: Statler Hotel, Boston.

AUDIENCE: Last year we had 900 in attendance which is about our average for the past five years. We have checked to see that there are no comparable events scheduled in Boston that evening, and we have been working toward having an audience of 1,000. Most are couples. There is a cross section of economic and vocational groups but most of those in attendance will be financial supporters of our Chapter from the business world.

DRESS: Black tie.

OTHER PRINCIPAL GUESTS: We always invite the Governor but past experience indicates he will not be able to accept. The Mayor, city officials, and a number of top civic leaders have always attended. We have invited our National President but if he comes he will make only some brief remarks and you would be the main speaker.

PUBLICITY: On the basis of previous years we can count on good advance and follow-up publicity in the local newspapers. If you do not use a prepared text we would like to have a few paragraphs of "excerpts" which can be furnished to newspapers. We also need six glossy print photos of you.

PRELIMINARIES AND TIME SCHEDULE: We will have a reception in advance at the same hotel, starting at 6:30 p.m. and ending at 7:30 p.m. We would want you to stand in the receiving line with the Chapter officers and the National President. The speaking will begin at 8:30 p.m. There will be six short talks and presentation of awards before you are introduced at 9:15 p.m.

POSSIBLE TOPICS: The speech should make reference to the Red Cross but it need not be about the Red Cross as such. You could talk about anything you care to.

ARRANGEMENTS: Your hotel room would be reserved and paid for by the local Chapter. A Chapter representative would meet you at the Airport and take you back to the Airport at the time of your departure.

Even if it is not feasible to furnish the sought-after speaker with all this information at the time the invitation is being extended, such a memorandum, in greater detail, should be prepared well in advance of the Dinner in order to be sure that nothing has been forgotten.

Don't Alienate Speaker

Care should be taken to see that the memorandum given to the invited speaker is friendly and gracious in tone and is not stuffy and didactic. For example avoid such instructions as: "Controversial topics should be avoided." "The size of the audience depends on the drawing power of the speaker." "It is essential that you be available for the receiving line promptly at 6:30 p.m. without fail."

The experienced speaker, looking over a memorandum such as that given above, will prepare himself for some almost certain departures from the hoped for plan. For example:

> If the National President does attend he will very likely be somewhat of a prima donna and it is unlikely he will limit himself to "brief remarks." Fifteen minutes is a fair guess as to the time he might take.
>
> If the Dinner is "black tie" on a week night it is very unlikely the reception will actually get under way at 6:30 and finish at 7:30. Many of the gentlemen will go home from the office, change into their tuxedoes, and pick up their wives. Parking and checking will cause delay.
>
> If there are to be "six short talks" before the main event the odds are heavy that at least one, and more probably two, of the preliminary speakers will become captivated by the sound of his own voice and will talk 12 to 15 rather than 2 to 3 minutes.

Speech Should Suit Occasion

Regardless of what the memorandum indicates, the speech theme in fact should tend to praise and glorify the work of the particular charity and its volunteer supporters. People like to be approved of. A dinner speech to a Red Cross annual dinner should be noncontroversial. It is not the time or place for making people angry.

In addition to the memorandum given to the speaker in the course of inviting him, further information should be sent to him, in one all-inclusive letter if possible, after he accepts and well in advance of the meeting.

Avoid P.A.L.L.

The program chairman, or whoever else is coordinating contacts with the speaker, should resolve, from

61

the first minute of the speaker's acceptance, to avoid P.A.L.L.: standing for "post acceptance liaison let-down."

Nearly every speaker, unless he is President of the United States, experiences P.A.L.L.

When he is being invited he is given the big build up. He is not only made to feel wanted—he is made to feel indispensable. Assuming—and this should always be the case—that he is a person who will add something to the program, the program chairman will almost inevitably resort to a certain amount of exaggeration, promotion, and flattery to induce the invited speaker to accept. Very often, if the prospect's acceptance would be something of a feather in the cap for the program chairman, the prospect is given the impression that the program will be a flop without him, that the success of the whole meeting revolves around him, and even that the organization may falter if he doesn't say "yes."

But even though the prospective speaker should discount a certain amount of the "big build up" it should be borne in mind that most highly desirable speakers are not shrinking violets. If they are on the "most wanted" list of program prospects they are likely to come from one of the following categories: 1. public officeholder with a big title; 2. top business or professional leader; 3. expert from academic or technical field who has something of special interest to say to the audience; 4. proven "motivator" in sales promotion, inspiration, patriotism, etc.; or 5. professional lecturer.

People from any one of these groups are likely, by heavy odds, to have done well in the competitive world.

They are highly likely to think they are important. This means they are susceptible to flattery—just like all the rest of us, except that in their case the flattery seems plausible.

IX

The Time Schedule

At most luncheons and dinners it takes too long to serve the meal and get rid of the waiters and their clatter.

At a charity event where I was to speak in California an overeager master of ceremonies announced at the *beginning* of the meal that the waiters should leave the room while we had the invocation. When they had left the minister, with a twinkle in his eye, said:

"I wasn't going to say anything they shouldn't hear."

The ideal situation on serving is the men's service club luncheon: Rotary, Kiwanis, and the like. When the guests arrive, the salad, rolls and butter, *and dessert* are already at each place. The waiters have only to serve the main dish, pour the coffee, and depart so that the speaking can and does begin in time for an unfailing 1:30 adjournment.

At luncheons where ladies are to be present or at evening dinners the "Rotary dessert" is not considered acceptable. More style and formality are indicated. But very often the time taken in serving and clearing the "first course," serving and clearing the entrée, serving and clearing the dessert, is the very time that can't be spared and which causes those present to look at their watches as the speaking progresses.

No luncheon should last beyond 2:00 at the very latest; no dinner should run later than 10:30.

Insist on Your Arrangements

It is vital that the chairman should lay down the law to the banquet manager of the hotel: after the dessert is served and the coffee poured, the waiters should get out and stay out! They should not pick up the dessert dishes.

Hotels do not like this system. While they have the waiters—usually part-timers—on duty, they want to use them to get all the dirty dishes back to the kitchen. They always insist it will not take extra time. But the truth is it adds ten minutes of clatter just when the guests are impatient to get on with the program.

The dinner chairman should also insist that pitchers of hot coffee and of ice water should be left on the tables before the waiters depart.

The time allowed for serving the meal depends on how many courses there are to be and this depends on whether the meal is really the main event or is just a side-line to the program. At a Rotary luncheon the meal is just an incidental. It may be an incidental at a political rally. On the other hand at a formal banquet winding up a three- or four-day convention the food, the service, and the sociability while eating are the important things. The speeches are only formalities.

The dinner chairman needs to analyze what his menu will require in terms of time for serving. If the waiters are to ladle out the soup from tureens for each guest individually, this will take more time than serving a fruit cocktail. So will tossed salad served by the waiters from bowls, or ice cream slices cut at each guest's place from a large, decorative cake of ice cream.

Under no circumstances attempt a self-service buffet at a luncheon or dinner where there is to be speaking. It takes forever for the line to wend its way past the various offerings. By the time the end of the line has gone through, the early birds have long since finished eating. They are either impatient for the speeches to start or else are complicating things further by going back for a second helping or for an extra dessert.

It is important not to allow a gap between the eating and the speechmaking. Once there is an appreciable delay the table hopping and the wandering out of the room will begin. Then more time is lost getting people back to their places.

Have a Meaningful Program

When setting up a luncheon or dinner the committee in charge and the toastmaster should carefully analyze the real purpose of the gathering to see what should have priority attention.

If the audience has come purely and simply because they want to hear a prominent person who is to give the main address, everything else should be subordinated to that address. Preliminary speeches should be dispensed with; no routine reports should be presented nor plaques or certificates awarded. The toastmaster should be brief and should not attempt to outdo Bob Hope. The introductions of the people at the head table should not attempt to give their entire pedigree.

If it is a large political fund raising dinner, the crowd, no matter who the speaker is, will have come primarily to see and be seen. The lobbyists and payrollers and hangers on will want to do some table hopping so that their political sponsors and the office holders can see that they are there. Speeches should be few, and short and peppy. Introductions should be brief. If there are paid entertainers, they should preferably be singers or musicians so that raucous demands for "quiet" are not necessary. In such a gathering food is secondary but decorations and music are important. A popular, humorous, and discreet toastmaster is all important. No attempt should be made to limit applause.

If it is a "recognition" event the person or persons to be recognized are all important. A banquet given by a sales organization to award trophies or plaques or certificates to sales leaders is a special type of gathering. The winning salesmen and their wives can never get enough of the spotlight and of ego recognition. A professional photographer should be provided to take pictures of each award winner receiving his trophy. A flash bulb going off adds to the big moment. And the awardee's wife should be given attention too—by having a corsage presented to her.

Too often a "boss," presiding at a dinner to honor a subordinate, such as a retiring employee, forgets who is the

67

guest of honor and uses much of the time to throw bouquets at himself.

If the event is a charity fund raising "report luncheon" it is important to let as many workers and leaders as possible get on their feet and tell what a great job they have been doing—but very briefly. Picture taking, door prizes, plaques, music—all are good for these events.

The Snarled Schedule

What should the main *speaker* do if the time schedule becomes so snarled that it is late in the evening and he still hasn't been called on?

This happened to the late Robert Millikan, the distinguished scientist, at a dinner in Los Angeles. He was supposed to be the main speaker but it was after 11 p.m. when he was introduced. He stood up unsmilingly, said it was time everyone was on his way home, and stalked out. It was a memorable slap at the careless and inept handling of the dinner. And Millikan had so much prestige he could get away with it. It is still being talked about in Los Angeles.

But for the ordinary mortal the only thing to do is grin and bear it. Otherwise the audience thinks the man is stuck on himself and that he has insulted them.

I remember a time schedule gone haywire at an insurance convention. Several months in advance I had been invited to be the main speaker. The program chairman contacted me every few weeks before the great event and gave me the impression I was supposed to deliver a landmark address. When I arrived at the convention hotel right on the dot at the appointed time of 12 noon the room where the luncheon was to be held was still cluttered with uneven rows of chairs for the morning panel session. The waiters were just beginning to roll into the room the large round luncheon tables. The printed program stated in boldface type that the next event for the entire convention was to start promptly without fail at 2 p.m. in *another room*.

I was finally called on for my 35 minute speech at five minutes before two!

I was not in the most buoyant of moods when I got to my feet. I was tempted just to tell a few jokes and sit down. But I realized a number of my good friends and boosters had come especially to hear me. So I gave about 20 minutes of the speech.

I should have given all of it. But I hadn't learned so well then that all you can do in such a situation is go along with it and not lose your temper. You can't win getting mad at a whole ballroom full of people.

In fact, whom *do* you blame? The person who actually sold you on coming and told you how indispensable you were, usually isn't in charge of other arrangements. (He wasn't that day—didn't let out a peep.) The M.C. may have been *told* he was to be the main performer. The arrangements committee may not know enough to ride herd on the hotel catering manager to be sure the room is set up in time.

One Source of Authority

That is why I say, for a good program one, and only *one*, forceful, knowledgeable man should be in complete charge (even if it is a big speaking event being put on by

69

a ladies' group). Then there is someone who has a continuing responsibility so that a dislocated time schedule won't make the much sought-after speaker feel like a skunk at a lawn picnic when the big moment arrives.

X

Making Humor
Seem Spontaneous

It is by no means necessary to be able to make up humor for the occasion in order to use the topical joke. In fact, unless you are absolutely positive that you really can make up jokes and humorous comments as you go along, don't try to innovate.

I have said before that if one is going to make speeches he should give speechmaking technique careful thought and attention—just as one who is going to play the violin in public should study and practice.

By the same token, if one is going to use humor in speeches, he should give *humor techniques* some thought and attention.

Be a Joke Collector

Most people do not remember jokes for long after they hear them. If you are going to use jokes in speeches you should develop a large inventory of humor so that you won't be chained to one or two stories but can pull out at the last minute whichever one of dozens has the most *pertinence.*

It is easy to build an inventory. Carry a pocket notebook and when you hear a good joke, write down a few key words from it then and there so that you can remember it later. Many good speakers do this. It has long been done by Hubert Humphrey, a speaker who has always been in great demand.

Organize and index your accumulation of jokes. A looseleaf or card file collection should have headings like "Preachers," "Salesmen," "Liquor," "Politicians."

Review your jokes so that you will have them in the back of your mind and can easily be reminded of the right one by a remark or incident, such as looking at the bulletin board in the hotel, which I mentioned in an earlier chapter. In that example, the speaker didn't make up the reference to a speech on $10,000 funerals. He had it in his mental file to be pulled out and used at the right time.

In fact he has many more "mortician" jokes in that mental file. "I hear that out at that fancy Forest Lawn Cemetery in Southern California they are having to put a big high fence around the place. . . . People are dying to get in."

Speakers Seek Topical Jokes

Nearly every speaker at least gropes for the audience appeal of a topical joke. Almost always there is an attempt—often awkward—to tie the joke to some incident or remark. "That reminds me of the story . . . ," the speaker often says. But usually nothing at all that has actually happened or been said even remotely reminds him of his joke. It is usually a joke which he brought with him to be told *regardless*.

Another type of topical humor is a remark or joke based on some news item or current subject of public discussion.

Here is an example of topical introductory material taken from the speech which I made to the Los Angeles Rotary Club on my last day in office as Postmaster General, August 9, 1963:

> Until recently my official residence has been in Los Angeles.
> Now I am pulling up stakes to practice law in the East.
> Not long ago another much better known public figure pulled up stakes in Los Angeles and moved East to practice law.
> However, Mr. Nixon and I have made the move for different reasons.
> Governor Pat Brown had nothing to do with *my* decision.
> I would have liked to have practiced law right here.
> But for an Illinois lawyer to get admitted to practice in California is as difficult as getting into Fort Knox.
> I just couldn't bring myself to go through those cram courses and bar exams again.
> And, anyway, there is already one lawyer for every 32

people in Beverly Hills, California—a statistic fully as startling to me as the fact that Los Angeles County is the largest milk producing county in the United States.

Most of the cows in the local feeding lots never saw a blade of grass.

They live on alfalfa pellets.

In more ways than one science is taking all the fun out of being a cow.

The press in Los Angeles has treated me kindly.

Mr. Nixon on the other hand thought they had treated him shabbily.

In fact last November he let it be known that he was holding his last press conference.

It has turned out to be the longest press conference in history.

It is still going on, all over Europe, with a new installment nearly every day.

Mr. Nixon may think he was given the shaft by the press.

But I, as a dedicated Democrat, have long been one of his most vocal publicizers.

For two years I have been predicting that he would be the Republican nominee for President again in 1964.

And the fact he has moved to New York doesn't alter my prediction one bit.

This will surprise many people because, after all, Mr. Rockefeller is already on the scene in New York.

And Mr. Rockefeller is a very smart man.

For example, it didn't take Rockefeller long to learn from Kennedy the advantage of having an Irish name in the family.

However, my guess, purely as a student of politics, is that the Republicans are going to decide they don't want to run another "me too" style New York governor—a sort of latter day Dewey—as their candidate.

And when that happens Rockefeller can then pass the ball to Mr. Nixon who will be conveniently available nearby.

Of course something might happen to throw Goldwater on the hopes of both of these gentlemen.

Admittedly, the oblique references to Governor Rockefeller's Mrs. Murphy, and to Nixon's surly press conference of November 1962, are dated now. But they were highly topical—and chuckle provoking—then.

Topical Jokes Are Surefire

In July of 1964 a joke about a topless bathing suit was bound to get a laugh. The month before that a joke about beagles' ears couldn't miss. (Plagiarism or simultaneous invention brought out references to "earlifts" all over the country.) And before the beagles, Billie Sol Estes and Bobby Baker had taken the place once occupied by deep freezers and vicuna coats as surefire topical joke material.

When using jokes tied to current events be sure to know your audience. A superinformed group such as those attending the annual Gridiron Dinner in Washington can be counted on to catch any tie-in to something that has been in the newspapers. But away from Washington and before groups who are not all ardent readers of newspapers, it pays to stick to the obvious references. In the Spring of 1964 a joke about putting more women in government would be understood anywhere. But the same would not be true about a dig at the "Ev and Charlie Show" because many reasonably well-posted people have never heard of that "show" (which is not really a TV show but a weekly news conference by the Republican leaders in Congress).

In the Spring of 1961 there was lots of mileage in the gag: "My brother-in-law has more consistent bad luck than anyone I know. I saw him just the other day. He was driving an Edsel with a Nixon bumper sticker on it, and his secretary is pregnant."

There were jokes, good natured and otherwise, about Eisenhower's golf and about Kennedy's religion.

One of the first type starts out picturing Ike as a superconscientious golfer who has a one track mind about the game. He is playing one day *incognito* at a course near Washington. On the fourteenth tee he takes several minutes as usual to get just the right stance and grip and to make some practice swings before his drive. But despite all the supercareful preparation he hooks and the ball arcs way over some trees and completely off the golf course.

He takes even longer on the next drive which goes straight and he and his companions finish the fourteenth and fifteenth and the rest of the holes. As they are walking back to the clubhouse they pass the fourteenth tee. A squad car is parked there and a policeman comes over to the unrecognized Ike.

"Did you drive from this tee about half an hour ago?" the policeman asks.

"Yes."

"Did you hook your ball way over those trees and off the course?"

"Yes, as a matter of fact I did."

"Do you know," continued the policeman belligerently, "your ball went out over the highway, cracked the windshield of a woman's car, she couldn't see where she was going, ran into a fire truck, the fire truck couldn't get to the fire, and a house burned down! . . . What are you going to do about it?"

Ike pondered a minute, picked up his driver, and said:

"Well, I think I'm going to open my stance a little and move my left thumb around further toward my right side."

XI

Humor Tied to the Location

A good form of topical humor at a convention is the joke about the area where the convention is being held.

In San Francisco the speaker might say:

"They have many ritzy suburbs around this city. There's one, called Atherton, that's so superexclusive even the fire department has an unlisted telephone number."

Or in Oklahoma City:

"You've heard about the dust bowl down this way and some of you have commented to me that this place seems to be pretty desperate for rain right at present. But if you think it's dry down here now you should have been here two years ago. It got so dry the Baptists were sprinkling, the Presbyterians were using a damp cloth, and the Episcopalians were giving rain checks."

Jokes about the area can, depending on the circumstances, the audience, and the sensitivity of the local hosts, pan the place where the meeting is being held—as for example, by indicating its local businessmen are sharp traders, hard bargainers, tight fisted, etc. The following could be used for Boston, Hartford, Cleveland, Detroit, or other big business centers.

Some Jokes about Places

A dashing and aristocratic boy from Mississippi joined the Army and was sent to a post near Boston for training before going overseas. He met an attractive Boston girl and in the course of a few weeks he became intimately acquainted with her.

A few months later, after he had been sent to Germany, he received a cablegram from her which read:

"I am with child. I am leaving for your ancestral home in Mississippi to await your happy return."

He immediately sent a reply cable:

"Stay where you are. A bastard has a better chance in Boston than a Yankee in Mississippi."

———•◦•———

And here is another story that goes over well, particularly with an audience in a Southern city.

A man from Detroit (Buffalo, etc.) was down here in Natchez on a business trip. When Sunday arrived he was out taking a walk and decided to go to church. Stop-

79

ping a colored man who was coming along the sidewalk he asked:

"Excuse me. What kind of a church is that over there?"

"It's a Baptist Church, sir."

"Good. I'm a Baptist. I'll just go right on over."

"Oh no, sir," said the Negro, "You don't want to go to *that* Baptist church."

"Why not?" asked our friend.

"Oh, because it's an *African* Baptist Church. The Baptist church *you* want to go to is about four blocks straight ahead, across the railroad tracks, and a block to the right."

"But this one is a Baptist church you said. What's the difference?"

"Well at *that* Baptist church that *you* want to go to they believes that Pharaoh's daughter discovered Moses in the bull rushes. And at this here Baptist church across the street they believe 'Dat's what *she* say!'"

Here's another one for use in a Southern or border state convention city.

A lady in Edinburgh whose youth was slipping away read in the paper that there were 20 per cent more women in Scotland than men—just not enough men to go around. So she moved to America and went to a woman friend in New Jersey to ask advice on seeking a husband.

"Well," said the friend, "in the North here you'll find the men are hard working and good providers. No monkey business about them—just nose to the grindstone and a good pay check come the end of the week. Now the Southern men are different. Not so educated—not so well

dressed—not so successful in business. But, oh, so roman-
tic. Charm all over the place. They treat you like a queen
—really know all about lovemaking. Now what are your
plans?"

The Scotslady thought it over. "I think I want a
Northern man from as far South as possible."

———•–•–•———

Here is one that can be used about a place the
speaker does not like:

I have been asked to announce the prizes in the big
national sales contest which starts next month. The first
prize will be a one week all expense stay in Toledo. The
second prize will be *two* weeks in Toledo.

———•–•–•———

Two men were standing on a street corner arguing
about how to pronounce "Hawaii."

"It's HA-VAH-EE," said one.

"No. No. It's HA-WAH-EE," said the other.

They argued on and on.

Finally the first man saw a stranger coming along.

"How do you pronounce Hawaii?" he asked.

"HA-VAH-EE," said the stranger.

"Ah, you're a very intelligent man. Thank you very
much."

"You're VELCOME," said the stranger.

———•–•–•———

An aristocratic lady from Boston, well along in
years, traveled to California some years ago to visit
friends. They took her to the proper places such as the
Huntington Art Gallery and various tea parties and DAR
meetings. At one such event a local citizen, trying to be
friendly, said:

81

"And how do you like Pasadena?"

"Oh, it's very lovely, and such nice, substantial people. But I find it hard to get used to being 3,000 miles from the ocean."

———•—•—•———

Another distinguished Boston lady met a young man at a dinner party in Beacon Hill.

"And where do you come from?" she asked.

"Iowa."

"Iowa? Where is *that*?"

"It's a big state, ma'am, out in the midwest."

"Oh, *that*. Back here we pronounce it *Ohio*."

———•—•—•———

XII

Reading a Speech

If you haven't learned how to "just talk" to an audience then, for Heaven's Sake—*read* to them!

A speech, even though read, can have audience appeal if certain simple rules are followed:

1. Don't sound bored with your material. Sound enthusiastic and peppy even if you have to force it. Don't drone.
2. Read the material through many times in advance.
   a) To be sure you know it well enough that you won't have

to puzzle or stumble over any sentence structures.

b) If there are any words or proper names you may
have trouble pronouncing you can practice them
and, as an added precaution, insert your own
phonetic spellings.

c) You can indicate on your text good spots for
pauses and emphasis—just as though you were
reading music.

d) You can mark paragraphs which could be omitted at the last minute if the time schedule gets
too tight.

3. Be sure the type is big enough and the podium light
is bright enough so you won't have to squint or
struggle over the text.

4. Double and triple check before you are called on to
be sure your pages are in order.

5. Don't pick up the pages as you finish them and lay
them obviously on the table beside the podium or
otherwise needlessly call attention to the fact you
are the captive of a typed text.

6. Never indicate, even as a "joke," that someone else
has ghostwritten the text.

7. At all costs, do not let copies of the prepared text
get into the hands of the audience in advance.

8. Look up from your text as often and as long as you
can without strain and without losing your place.

Lyndon Johnson's Set-up

Lyndon B. Johnson, who has made thousands of
speeches over the years, takes no chances on the physical
set-up for a speaking appearance. Starting long before

he was Vice President or President he has always insisted that the podium from which he is to speak must be exactly 42 inches above the floor—no more, no less. He knows that at his height and with his particular glasses, this gives him the best possible vision for his notes or his text. During my term in public office in Washington I noted on many occasions the unfailing care of his staff in checking the podium well in advance of the arrival of the audience.

They also checked the microphone and podium lights and, since its development, they dust off the glass speech text reflector.

The best method for de-emphasizing a prepared text is to have the speech typed doublespaced on 5 x 8 inch bond paper or cards, which can be attached together by ring binders across the top. Then the pages can be flipped up and over as each one is finished. The front of the podium will screen the turning of these half size pages, and the binder guarantees that the pages will not accidentally get mixed up so that they are out of order.

The purpose is not to fool the audience into thinking the speech is not being read. They well know it if they have occasion to think about it. But there is no point in reminding them with every new page. And any distraction interferes with audience attention.

Prepare Your Speech

Senator Olin Johnston of South Carolina was once speaking on foreign aid from a ghostwritten text he had not read in advance. Apparently the ghost-writer had not bothered to find out from past speeches that the Senator was against foreign aid. Johnston read along from the text with emphasis and gestures. After he had finished one key paragraph, he stopped abruptly, silently read through the paragraph again and then burst out excitedly:

"I don't agree with that *at all!*"

There is a story of a business tycoon who doted on making ghostwritten speeches to chambers of commerce and service clubs. His speech writer was good and the tycoon received many invitations. But he didn't want the writer to demand more money, so after every speech, no matter how well received, he berated the writer and told him the text was terrible.

One day the tycoon was speaking before a top level national convention of business leaders. He delivered several pages of the text and read to the audience the following from the bottom of page 6:

"And now I want to give to you ten specific steps that should be taken to halt the balance of payments gap and the gold drain."

Beaming with self-esteem he turned to page 7. It was a complete blank except for the words:

"O.K. big shot—you're on your own!"

One time when I was to speak before a prestige group of business men at a luncheon at the Waldorf Astoria, I reluctantly agreed to use a prepared text, for press release purposes, but I intended to depart from it freely and liven up the talk with ad libbing. A local press aide who had never worked with me put me on the spot with some eager beaver stupidity. When I arrived for the luncheon I found to my horror that a mimeographed copy of the speech had been placed on each guest's plate where it could be read at least half an hour before I was even to be called on. This was a new, unexpected hazard in using a canned text. I decided to get the benefit of two messages to this important audience and made an entirely different speech, off the cuff.

On an official trip to Japan I found an adaptation of this system was very helpful in crossing the language barrier. On two formal speech occasions the Embassy had thoughtfully provided individual copies of my speech, translated into Japanese, at each guest's place.

XIII

Talking to Salesmen

Use of humor in speeches to salesmen is of special importance. Salesmen like jokes. They do not like complicated and technical lectures. Many conventions are reward or recognition sessions for successful salesmen. This means the audience has come to be complimented and amused rather than to be enlightened or worried.

There are endless ways for the speaker to weave in stories about selling and salesmen. Here is a favorite, about the "world's greatest salesman," which I first heard from Chuck Luckman, the world famous architect, who, while still in his twenties, became the "boy wonder" of the promotional business world as a toothpaste company executive.

A man came into a men's clothing store and told the manager he wanted a job as a salesman.

"I don't need any salesmen," said the manager brusquely.

"Oh, but I'm not just any salesman. I'm the world's greatest salesman. You've *got* to hire me!"

Again the manager refused impatiently. But the man was insistent and persuasive, emphasizing that he was, without doubt, the world's greatest salesman.

"OK," said the manager, at last. "I'll tell you what. See that suit over there on the rack? It's sort of a green and purple plaid, with padded shoulders, sharp lapels, and a belt in the back. I don't know how I ever got stuck with it. It's been hanging there for two years. Now I'm about to go out to lunch. I'll leave you here and if you can sell that suit while I'm gone, you're hired."

In about an hour the manager came back. To his horror the store was a shambles. The show cases were turned over, the carpeting was ripped up, the chandeliers were hanging from frayed wires, and merchandise was strewn all over the floor. But the suit was gone!

Recovering himself the manager said:

"I see you sold the suit!"

"Yep," said the salesman proudly.

"But you seem to have had quite a bit of trouble with the customer!"

"Nope. No trouble at all with the customer—but, oh, that seeing eye dog!"

How to Get Leads

In any speech to salesmen it is appropriate to talk about how to get leads to prospects. Familiar devices include direct mail return cards, birth announcements

89

(for life insurance sales), personal referrals, and repeat customers. This difficult aspect of selling is of intense concern to every salesman.

Here is a pertinent story:

> Ryan asked Clancy to go to the horse races but Clancy insisted he had to go to confession.
>
> "All right," said Ryan, "I'll go along and wait for you outside."
>
> In the confessional Clancy admitted that he had committed adultery.
>
> "Was it that Mrs. Flanagan?" said the priest.
>
> "No, father," said Clancy.
>
> "Was it Mrs. Murphy?"
>
> "No, father."
>
> "Mrs. O'Hoolehan?"
>
> "No."
>
> When Clancy came out of the church Ryan asked:
>
> "Well, did you get forgiveness for your sins?"
>
> "No. But I got a lot of good leads."

I once heard a successful salesman explain in a humorous way how he got leads. His company sent out direct mail advertising which promised those sending in their names that they would receive, absolutely free, a handsome ballpoint pen and, said the advertisement, "NO SALESMAN WILL CALL." Our friend got hold of a stack of the returned cards and went out to deliver the pens in person and to do some selling.

At the first house the woman who answered the door was indignant and reminded him of the statement on the circular that said, "NO SALESMAN WILL CALL."

"Ma'am," he said, in a disarming and innocent way, "I'm the nearest thing to no salesman our company has."

Keep It Simple

Speeches to salesmen involve endless repetition of a few well-worn themes: hard work, perseverance, confidence, familiarity with product, enthusiasm, planning. Selling is a "mood" vocation. The salesman must be kept buoyed up, flattered, egged on, encouraged. It doesn't do to talk to him too much about problems and complications and difficulties. Everything should be optimistic, positive thinking. It is unwise to remind the salesman that there are all kinds of governmental and competitive hurdles which might give him an excuse for not making sales.

Keep It Lively

With these necessary repetitions of familiar, simple themes, it is important for the speaker not to seem bored with his subject, droning out bromides. Stories about selling are particularly important to give freshness and variety to the well-worn slogans about how to sell. A lengthy lecture purely in generalities and high-sounding phrases, about perseverance in selling, would put a roomful of salesmen to sleep.

But, with a proper lead in, a story such as this one drives home the importance of refusing to take no for an answer.

> Molly McGinnis was in love with John and he with her, but Molly confided to her mother, John was a Baptist and very much against marrying a Catholic. Molly was all in tears.
> "Now Molly," said Mother McGinnis. "Let's use some salesmanship about this. John's an intelligent lad. You just sit down and talk to him about our great church. Explain to him about its long history, about its being the first of all the Christian religions, tell him about its great beliefs and about

the brave martyrs and the noble saints and the wonderful cathedrals and the beauty of the service. Now go along and give him a good selling job."

Molly dried her eyes and went out on a date with John. Mother McGinnis waited eagerly—and confidently. But later in the evening Molly could be heard sobbing loudly even before she got in the house. The mother rushed to comfort her.

"What's the matter," she asked, "didn't you sell him?"

"Sell him!" sobbed Molly, "I *oversold* him. He wants to become a priest!"

Salesmen: an American Institution

My comments about speaking to salesmen should not be misunderstood. True, I don't pretend to think salesmen are intellectuals who thrive on original thinking about the great and complex issues of our time. I wouldn't expect to see nearly as many of them attending Great Books Courses as prize fights and poker games. I wouldn't expect them to read Walter Lippmann before Li'l Abner.

But they are far more important in our society than many realize. Selling on commission is a uniquely free enterprise activity. Laying bricks, or taking out an appendix, or installing a telephone can be and is done just as typically in a Communist society where everyone works for the Super State as in a free, private-ownership society.

But a Super State *doesn't* use selling and salesmen. It plans and regiments and rations and doles. But it has no place for the salesman in its distribution system.

The Super State does not rely on promotion and advertising and merchandising except for narrow propaganda purposes. In Japan the government uses 70,000 men as collectors for its state run life insurance system. But they are not independent small businessmen working under an incentive compensation system as are American life insurance *salesmen* (they prefer to be called "life underwriters").

Be Complimentary

Speeches to salesmen should build up the man who sells as the epitome of what is distinctive and worth preserving about our American free enterprise system. This isn't just flattery. It is true. More people should realize it.

Members of every vocation crave recognition and dignity and salesmen deserve far more of these than they receive. Too often the public's image of the salesman is of a pest with his foot in the door. So I prefer that the jokes I tell to salesmen be about selling situations and that they not ridicule and stigmatize salesmen as such. Our modern day successful salesman is a far different creature than the traveling salesman who figured in Pullman smoker jokes. The old time drummer was often the exploiter, the seducer, the cheap fly-by-night tinhorn. Salesmen today, for such firms as IBM, are top flight professional men, highly ethical and technically knowledgeable.

Humor with a Point

In talking to salesmen, humor can be used to get across instructions and warnings, which might seem offensive if delivered straight. No salesman should drink at lunch time. But if a speaker says that he may seem sanctimonious; instead, he might much better lead in by telling the group about the sales manager of a big company who became concerned because his salesmen were doing so much drinking at noon. He called them all together one morning and made this statement:

> Gentlemen, a number of you have asked me about whether we have a company policy on drinking at noon time. I have made an inquiry on this to the home office and here are the rules. Since we are a distinguished company with a fine reputation to keep up, it is important to follow these rules scrupulously. You salesmen can feel free to drink before lunch all the whiskey you want and also any beer, wine, or cocktails. But there is to be absolutely no drinking of vodka. . . . We want our customers to know you are drunk and not think you are stupid.

Be Carefully Didactic

For most speaking occasions, where the speaker is tempted to exhort an audience of salesmen with advice and words of wisdom, the old gag is a sound warning: "If you want to deliver a message—call Western Union."

However, many messages can be delivered painlessly and effectively by use of humorous stories that have an undertone of truth. People will listen to stories where they will not listen to preaching.

The parable was a very successful message form at least 2,000 years ago. Many a truth is spoken in jest— and better so.

This all adds up to a mighty challenge to the speaker to be interesting and if at all possible, entertaining. Humor within the body of the speech helps to jog the attention of the listeners. And it helps them to enjoy the speech—which means not only that they remember something of what is said, but remember the speaker favorably so that they would like to hear him again.

Comic Speeches

Some speakers popular with groups of salesmen have, in their eagerness to hold the attention of the audience, practically abandoned any semblance of normal speechmaking and turned instead to a technique close to a vaudeville act. Mr. Harold Stewart, for years a brilliant executive vice president of Prudential, transformed himself, when he appeared before large agents' conventions, from a no-monkey-business leader to a boisterous business barker with a huge bag of tricks. All manner of gadgets and gimmicks, props and flash cards were used in his talks. At one point he used a kitchen broom to drive practice golf balls into the audience.

Such surprises can always be woven into a sales talk by way of illustrating salient points the speaker wants to make. The golf ball routine was to drive home the point that you can't get good results without the right equipment, i.e., a salesman can't sell unless he has the right products.

I remember another of Stewart's gimmicks built around the theme that good promotion can make a success even of a hard to sell product. Stewart claimed that for years there had been no market for the meat of a certain large, ugly fish with a strange, technical name. The fish were plentiful and tasted all right but no one would eat them. With that, Stewart produced from behind a screen an outsized, multicolored papier mâché fish with a bulbous body, a leering face, and disgusting appendages. Next he produced an enormous poster card bearing an unpronounceable technical name. It was easy for the audience to understand why no one would want to eat such a creature with such a name.

Then he elaborated on the importance of imaginative sales promotion. As a climax he explained that some inspired soul thought of calling the fillets of this ugly fish "ocean perch" instead of the forbidding technical name. Immediately neat cellophane packages of these fillets were top sellers in supermarkets.

Using Props

Jim Rutherford, another top life insurance executive, also made effective use of props in his sales pep talks. His frequent theme was that life insurance coverage, as supplied by Prudential, provided the ultimate essentials: bread, meat, and potatoes. Behind him as he spoke was what appeared to be a model of Prudential's trademark, the Rock of Gibraltar, covered with a cloth. Jim referred to the Rock frequently during his "bread, meat, and potatoes" speech. At the end he dramatically pulled off the cloth and revealed that "Gibraltar" was in fact a huge ham, a loaf of bread, and a sack of potatoes.

At a convention in Sun Valley, I saw a sales manager from Ogden, Utah hit the jackpot with a speech theme illustration in vaudeville style. His talk was on planning —that the seemingly impossible could be done with sufficient advance planning and preparation.

"For example," he said, "anyone knows a man can't take his shirt off without first removing his coat."

While he continued patter along this line he undid his tie, unbuttoned his shirt front and cuffs, all the time leaving his coat on. Then at the key moment he grabbed the back of his shirt collar, gave a yank, and off came the shirt leaving him with his coat over his undershirt. The audience howled.

I was to speak to the same group as the final speaker the next day and I decided to go him one better. I found out that the secret of the trick was to rip the shirt open up each side to the sleeve and to lay the sleeves on top of the arms, without putting the arms in them. Then when the collar and cuffs and shirt front are buttoned and the coat is put on no one can tell the shirt isn't being worn in a normal way.

As I approached the end of my speech the next day, I reminded the audience of the previous day's talk on planning and the shirt incident.

"But some planning is incomplete," I extemporized. "Some preparation does not go far enough to achieve the maximum result."

With that I began unbuttoning my shirt.

"Imagination and ingenuity are vital in making the most of planning," I continued. "Did you notice that after yesterday's speaker so cleverly and surprisingly removed his shirt while his coat was still on, he was left standing there in his undershirt? Very untidy. Very undignified."

With that, I pulled my unbuttoned shirt from the back of my coat collar and stood there neatly attired in another dress shirt and tie which I was wearing underneath all the time.

I had no trouble with the two-minute listening span.

Humor Drives Home Point

Aside from its value in jogging the attention of listeners, humor in the body of a speech is highly valuable as a way of driving home a point. Usually, of course, as in the case of Harold Stewart's props, the humor serves the dual purpose of regaining attention and illustrating a theme. But even with a highly attentive audience a humorous story can make a point remembered when nothing else will.

For example, with no props or vaudeville the following story, told as true (it might be) drives home Stewart's point that clever promotion can move even a hard to sell product.

> Clancy and Ryan discovered a place on the West Coast that abounded in salmon and they put all the money they had saved or could borrow into building a huge salmon cannery with all the latest machinery. When thousands of cases had been canned, labeled, and shipped it was discovered that the salmon from the cans was pure white and that housewives, used to pink salmon, wouldn't buy it. Clancy and Ryan were faced with ruin. They changed the process but the salmon was still white. Just as bankruptcy proceedings were about to begin, Ginsburg came along and told them that for $50,000 he would tell them how to sell all their salmon. They borrowed more money and met his price.
>
> "It's simple," he said. "Just print prominently on every label: 'This salmon positively guaranteed not to turn pink in the can.' "

Imaginative promotion. Supersalesmanship. Such a story can illustrate several familiar speech themes.

The "True" Story

Bart Lytton, the brilliant West Coast savings and loan executive, uses this "true" story to poke fun at financial giants who take advantage of the little man.

> An ignorant sheepherder was faced with the loss of his flock during an unusually severe winter when no food was

available. He finally was forced to go into town and for the first time in his life he entered the bank and asked to borrow $400 to buy feed.

The banker was tough:

"We don't know anything about you. Before we'll let you have any money you'll have to put up security. How many sheep have you got?"

The banker took a mortgage on all the sheep. Most other herders lost their flocks and the price of sheep was high in the spring. Our sheepherder sold his flock for $4,000. He went to the bank to pay back the $400 and as he was leaving the banker asked where he was going next.

"Back to the mountains."

The banker showed great concern.

"You mustn't go up there by yourself with all that money on you. You will be robbed."

"What else can I do?"

"Leave your money with us," said the banker.

The sheepherder looked at him coldly.

"How many sheep have *you* got?" he asked.

Anecdotes, true stories, and could-be true stories are particularly useful in the body of speeches. They provide a change of pace, and a subtle means of emphasis.

A frequent subject of speeches to business groups is that business is far more regulated and hamstrung than are unions, that business concerns are under the antitrust laws while unions are not, and that unions have great political power so that they receive kinder treatment from legislative bodies than does business. Such a theme can be pointed up by the following story:

A high-pressure business executive developed insomnia. As he lay in bed his mind churned with all the pressing business problems and negotiations of the day just passed. Morn-

99

ing came and he was fagged and jittery. One sleepless night succeeded another and in the meantime his problems at the office got worse. He went to his doctor and asked for a prescription for sleeping pills. The doctor gave him something that he assured him would do the trick. But another week of sleepless nights followed and he was back at the doctor's again. The doctor gave him something stronger and warned him to be careful in taking it. But a week later the business man was back again—still sleepless and with the dark circles under his eyes bigger than ever.

"Doctor," he pleaded, "you've got to do something. This is driving me crazy, and my company is going to the dogs. I've got to get some sleep and none of those pills you've given me have done a bit of good. What's this I hear about some doctors using something called 'twilight sleep'?"

"Why," smiled the doctor, "that's just for labor."

"But doctor," groaned the man, "don't you have *something* for *management?*"

You certainly can't sell successfully unless you like selling. But you can't tell if you like it unless you try it and you have to try it long enough to give yourself a chance to like it. To illustrate:

An American was alone on a dreary night in the lounge of an English club. Hoping to strike up a conversation with a distinguished looking Britisher sitting nearby he said:

"May I buy you a drink?"

"No," said the Britisher coolly. "Don't drink. Tried it once and didn't like it."

Nothing daunted the American offered him a cigarette.

"No. Don't smoke. Tried it once and didn't like it."

"Then how about a little game of cribbage?"

"No. Don't play cribbage. Tried it once and didn't like it. But my son will be dropping by after a bit. He might want to play."

100

The American settled back in his chair.
"Your only son, I presume."

Speeches to salesmen can make use of a variety of attention-holding gimmicks.

For example, the speaker might say:

Alaska is the largest State in the Union in area. Texas is second. Now where do you think Pennsylvania ranks in area? In the course of my speech, I am going to be using some numbers. If you think Pennsylvania ranks fourth **and** you hear me use the number four, jump to your feet as soon as I say it. Everyone who jumps up on the wrong number will have to sit down again, put his unfolded handkerchief over his head, and leave it there until there is a correct answer. The first one to jump up on the correct number will receive a box of a dozen golf balls.

Then all kinds of valuable facts and statistics can be included in the speech and everyone will listen. Nearly everyone will have a handkerchief on his head before the speaker says:

"And in the latest survey of the familiarity of housewives with the name of our product, we found only 34 who had never heard of it."

The first one up on 34 is the winner.

At a national convention of a big sales organization which I attended, the main banquet speaker was a smartly dressed and highly articulate "Polish Countess" who told about her experiences as a spy. The first ten minutes or so was completely straight and credible. Then, almost imperceptibly, slightly wacky comments crept in. The listeners began to glance at each other and it was some time before, one by one, they realized it was a hoax. Finally off came the wig. It was a professional and highly skillful comedian.

XIV

Charity Functions

Humor is particularly appropriate at charity functions. There are three types of such events:

1. Fund raising dinners where potential contributors are gathered so they can be exhorted to give.
2. "Report luncheons" to hear progress reports from the workers in a fund raising campaign.
3. Annual dinners of permanent charitable groups, given to arouse interest among workers and donors. The annual Boy Scout, YMCA, and Red Cross dinners are examples.

All these have a serious purpose. But people will be sorry they came if all they hear are pleas for funds, stories of need, pep talks, and repetitious build up of the organization or the work done. Propaganda palls, even if for a good cause.

Avoid Controversy

On the other hand, these events must necessarily steer clear of controversy. The purpose is to put those in the audience in a good mood—not to make them mad. That is one danger of using a professional at such a gathering.

When I lived in Los Angeles, I attended the annual dinner of a major charity of which I was a member of the Board of Directors. The speaker was a high-powered pro who makes scores of speeches a year to all kinds of groups all over the country for sizable fees. His technique was to string together a series of anecdotes (some supposedly true), personal and funny experiences, and jokes. His underlying framework was right wing and antigovernment.

He belittled federal policies with ridiculous examples. Most of those in the audience were from the conservative business stratum and the speaker went over big, especially since he did have a great many funny stories.

However, to a more sensitive member of the Democratic Party than myself, he could have been very offensive because some of his material was highly partisan. After the speech the executive secretary of the organization, conscious of my active political affiliation, apologized to me for having to sit still through so much slanted talk. I passed it off.

At another charity dinner in Los Angeles the speaker came up with this one.

A man reputed to be very wealthy never gave a cent to charity. An eager beaver working on a hospital drive resolved to break through this stone wall. By talking to a number of people he got extensive information on the man's income and assets. Then he went to the man's office and after his heartrending sales talk said:

"I understand you have some half million dollars in stocks, a million dollars in bonds, and hundreds of thousands of dollars worth of real estate. Your stocks have doubled in value in just the past year and you have struck oil on your property in Texas."

The man said politely:

"You have obviously done a lot of research on me. I'm impressed. You know a great deal about me. But you didn't say anything about my brother in Colorado."

"Your brother?"

"Yes. He lost his job about a year ago, he can't find another, his house has been foreclosed, and he and his wife and six children are absolutely down and out and have no one to turn to but me."

The man continued:

"And you didn't say anything about my sister."

"Your sister?"

"Yes. She's been sick and crippled up for years. Can't even pay her doctor bills. Has to live in one little rented room above a store. Has no one to turn to but me."

The man went on in the same vein telling about the miseries and poverty of his old father, an uncle, and a niece. With that the embarrassed fund raiser arose apologetically.

"I'm sorry I didn't know about all of them. What you've told me helps me to understand why you turned us down."

"Good. I thought it would," said the man. "I don't give a dime to any of them so I don't see why you expect me to help you."

A Good Canned Joke
Can Work

President Kennedy seldom used canned jokes but in a speech to a labor convention in Miami he told this old but good one using as his foil Arthur Goldberg, who was then Secretary of Labor.

> Goldberg went mountain climbing and got lost. After he had been missing some time a rescue party headed up the mountain to look for him. It was getting dark and the head of the rescue party shouted:
> "Goldberg, Goldberg, it's the Red Cross."
> A voice came back from higher up the mountain.
> "I already gave at the office."

One "out of the same card file" involves two Frenchmen who similarly went mountain climbing in the Alps and were suddenly buried up to their necks in snow by an avalanche. Just when they were about to give up hope of rescue, a St. Bernard was seen coming toward them with a little barrel of brandy tied under his neck.

One of the men shouted.

"Ah. Thank God! Here comes man's best friend. And look at that enormous dog that's carrying it!"

Movies and Slides Effective

Short movies and slide films about the organization's work and interesting or appealing case histories can be used effectively at charity functions.

The important thing at a charity event is to bring the audience close to the problem. Get them involved. Privation and misfortune can be ignored if they are distant and the victims are strangers. On the other hand, most anyone would lend a hand to his next door neighbors if they were victims of misfortune.

The speaker at a charity event should try to give the listeners that "next door neighbors" sense of commitment.

The following is a speech that I used to drive home that message. The speech text itself is not intended to be humorous but I preceded it with several appropriate and topical jokes.

"Don't Live on Austin Street"

The title of my talk is "Don't Live on Austin Street."

This does not mean I am going to make a real estate pitch in reverse.

It does not mean I have had some unpleasant experience on Austin Street or that I have had trouble with some person who lives there. As a matter of fact, I don't know anyone who lives on that street.

Austin Street is quiet and respectable. It is part of one of the better neighborhoods with homes in the $35,-000 to $60,000 price range.

It is a real street inhabited by real people, living in private homes and apartment buildings.

But it is also a symbol.

I have friends who live on the symbolic Austin Street. Sometimes I have tarried there myself. It is easy to stay there forever. I have moved on, but somehow more and more people seem to be living there. They seem to be quite satisfied with living there.

Austin Street is a street in Kew Gardens in New York City.

There, late one night in the spring of 1964, a young

woman named Catherine Genovese was stabbed on the street in three separate attacks by a lurking assailant. Twice the attacker was temporarily frightened away, so that 30 minutes elapsed between the first attack and the third one. After the third attack, Catherine Genovese was dead.

If that had been all there was to the incident it would have been forgotten by now. The thing that makes it unforgettable and incredible is that while the three separate attacks were taking place, 38 different people living in the neighborhood watched from their windows and did nothing.

During the hideous half hour not one of the 38 even lifted the telephone from the safety of his own apartment to call the police.

Later detectives went knocking at the doors of the 38 asking why they had watched but done nothing. Most of the 38 were quite matter of fact about their role— not particularly embarrassed or ashamed. They explained that they just didn't want to get involved.

A woman in the neighborhood said:

"Let's forget the whole thing. It is a quiet neighborhood, good to live in. What happened, happened."

Only one of the 38 witnesses finally did anything about calling the police—35 minutes after the first attack, and after Catherine Genovese was already dead. He first phoned a friend in another county for advice and then crossed the roof of a building to the apartment of an elderly woman and asked her to phone the police.

There has been wide publicity about this incredible display of civic irresponsibility and lack of compassion. Psychiatrists, "behavioral specialists," and ordinary citizens are still trying to figure out how this could have happened in our United States.

Lack Conscience

I am not saying that any one of the 38 should have rushed out and engaged the lurking murderer in personal combat.

But on the real Austin Street the desire to avoid becoming involved was so paralyzing it ruled out even a safe, anonymous telephone call. It revealed a shocking lack of conscience toward humanity and the community. It revealed also the depersonalizing and dehumanizing even of affluent people in our modern society.

Austin Street is a symbol of apathy. It is a symbol of shirking indifference toward one's fellow man.

We like to think, and with good reason, that the very best in American character is associated with our rural tradition. We recall stories of a farm house that burned down and of loyal neighbors turning out voluntarily to rebuild it. We think of democratic government in its most personalized form being practiced in town meetings in country communities. We think of great American leaders born in log cabins or developing strong principles and strong backbones tilling the soil or working long hours in country stores.

But whether we like it or not—and personally I do not like it at all—we have been observing the gradual liquidation of rural America. We have seen the trend to fewer and much larger farms. We have seen the shriveling up and disappearance of many of our little country towns. Back in 1890, when Adlai Stevenson's grandfather was Assistant Postmaster General of the United States, there were 70,000 separate post offices in the United States, mostly in small villages. Today there are less than half that many.

When our country was young only 5 per cent of the population lived in places of 2,500 or more population. Today two out of every three persons live in the larger towns and cities and in the huge urban areas.

By the end of this century, in only 36 years, the population of this country is expected to double to 350 million people, and most of these people will be living in cities.

Two hundred years ago in his great poem, "The Deserted Village," Oliver Goldsmith bemoaned the passing of an era when each citizen worked his own little plot of land and lived a life free of materialism. He would indeed moan if he could see the teeming neon jungles of our cities today.

Not long ago a friend of mine said to me:

"I have just been out to Los Angeles. I have seen the future—and it won't work."

Involvement Necessary

Too often we convince ourselves that our responsibilities to our less fortunate fellow men are fully met by welfare programs carried on for us at an antiseptic distance by government employees. But government cannot and should not do the whole job. The war on poverty, for example, must be broader than just a government program. That war must be fought in large part by volunteers. Isn't a dedicated volunteer with his individual effort among the poor and ignorant, a nobler example of altruism than an impersonal, highly staffed program conducted entirely with government funds? Wouldn't each of us be more successful as human beings if we joined first hand, on the front lines, in efforts to alleviate destitution? It would not only show that we cared, but also that we were willing to become involved.

The dwellers on Austin Street were not only timid and callous about a human life; they were also indifferent and cringing about their responsibilities to support law and order. We read every few weeks of attacks on police taking place while supposedly decent citizens stand by doing nothing. We hear people rationalize violence and disorder and riot on the ground that they are in support of a good cause. We see our law enforcement officials thrown on the defensive in many areas by civil liberties fanatics and bleeding hearts who want to create an increasingly impossible obstacle course for police. We hear impractical demands for civilian review boards to backseat drive and hamstring police departments.

And much of this happens because there are so many decent citizens who sit back and say, "I don't want to become involved."

In many parts of the world, in new democracies, 90 and 95 per cent of those eligible turn out to vote in elections. In many towns in India, for example, 100 per cent of the voters consistently turn out. But here in our country, the oldest democracy in the world, at every national election tens of millions of citizens do not take the trouble to vote. They are apathetic and indifferent. They do not bother to become involved.

We need to duplicate today some of the personal, individual, unselfish involvement in government which typified the town meeting of the past. Otherwise, we turn our public life over to cynical manipulators who believe that politics is just a game—a game played only to win at any price and by any means—without regard to principle and idealism.

We must never retreat so far up Austin Street that we say:

"Politics is all bad and I don't want to get involved in it. I will stay at a safe distance and leave it to the calloused professionals."

People of good will and integrity must be concerned with what they can do for their country and their community. Government at all levels needs people who care.

A dweller on the symbolic Austin Street might say:

> I am very advanced and altruistic in my social thinking. I have discarded the old ideas of survival of the fittest. I even realize that in our incredibly complex society many men cannot be masters of their own economic destiny, and self-reliance is not always enough. But I am not my brother's keeper. The government is his keeper. I am not responsible if respect for law is diminishing. That is a problem for the police. I am not responsible if the total community is becoming a hideous and disorderly sprawl. I will move out into the suburbs and leave all that behind. I do not want to become involved.

What do you say to such a person who does not care?

What do you say to one who sneers at the old, traditional ideals and sense of personal responsibility?

It is not so much what you say as what you—as a dedicated and enlightened person—do by way of example. In any generation there are certain solid elements who are the opinion leaders—who hold in trust the ideals and the conscience of the community and the society.

Community Conscience

It is the conscience of the community that brings us together here tonight. We are here because we are ready, willing and eager to become involved in a vital civic responsibility—the United Appeal.

Let us leave this meeting determined not to be begrudging, reluctant or apathetic about this year's drive. Let us be evangelists and true believers, ready to meet and vanquish those who say:

"Oh, is it that darn United Appeal time again."

"I'm too busy to take part."

"I gave at the office."

"Let the government do it."

Let us determine that this great and necessary drive will not be impersonal and anonymous and insulated. Let us have some face-to-face contact with those who benefit from these funds and urge others to do the same. Let us not solicit and sign pledge cards merely as an irksome chore we don't know how to get out of. Let us take part because we know about and believe in the Federated Charities, the Children's Aid Society, the Red Cross and the Salvation Army and seven other agencies which serve you and Frederick County.

There are compensations for the person who is willing to become involved. He is part of the mainstream of life. He avoids that deadly peril of our well-fed society —boredom. Advancing technology is providing increased leisure time. Leisure that is devoted entirely to play or to idleness soon begins to pall. But leisure time devoted to being involved in selfless service to others enhances the significance of life.

The slogan of the cynic is "Never Volunteer." The warning of the timid soul is "Don't Stick Your Neck Out." The watchword of the pseudo-sophisticate is "Don't Be an Eager Beaver." The sneer of the scoffer is "So What? Who Cares?"

But the cynics and the timid souls and the pseudo-sophisticates and the scoffers are not the ones who savor the zest and excitement of life. They remain on the sidelines—inert, cautious, uncommitted. They are only spectators of the great forward march of human kind.

The self-centered, indifferent attitude of Austin Street is not a new problem. The people who took the other side of the road to avoid the man who was eventually helped by the Good Samaritan were presumably average, typical people of their day, 20 centuries ago.

But in every age we need to be reminded that "God is Love"—that the deepest human satisfaction comes from personal concern for one's fellow man.

We need to have the courage to be willing to become involved.

We need to keep telling ourselves "Don't live on Austin Street."

———•••———

At an Israel Bond Drive dinner, I heard this story:

> The master of ceremonies at a fund raising dinner waited until the crucial moment to make his high-pressure pitch for contributions. He exhorted members of the audience to stand and announce their pledges. Finally after he had pulled out all the stops a man rose and said:

"I'm Morris Sachs of Sachs Furniture Company. I pledge $1,000."

Another man rose.

"I'm Ben Kaufman of Acme Restaurants. I pledge $2,000."

After each pledge the orchestra played a fanfare and the M.C. continued his high-powered appeal. There were more and more contributors.

Finally a man rose in the back of the hall:

"I'm Abe Ginsburg, owner of Abe Ginsburg Men's Furnishings Store, 3098 West Jefferson Street, next to the Orpheum Theatre. Free parking in the rear, easy credit terms, free alterations. I pledge $25 anonymously!"

Another story illustrates the bad attitude of some people toward charity.

A whale and a herring had long been inseparable. Then one day the other creatures in the sea saw the herring alone and asked where his great friend the whale was. The herring replied: "How should I know? I'm not my blubber's keeper!"

XV

Humor Tied to the News

For an afterdinner speech, where humor is to be the main ingredient, much can be done with humor tied to current news items.

The speech can be couched in mock serious language as though it were a genuine discussion of foreign affairs, politics, or Congress. This approach allows the speaker to poke fun at communists, politicians, foreign aid, high taxes, "bureaucrats," congressional junkets, and a great many other things that audiences like to hear ridiculed.

This type of humor appears in daily syndicated columns by such writers as Art Buchwald, Art Hoppe, and George Dixon. (Their problem is they have to "be funny" too often.)

The Ridiculous Twist

Some serious points can be covered, camouflaged by imaginary and exaggerated imitations of genuine news. In addition, nearly every day's newspaper contains a report of some actual incident that has a ridiculous twist. Reading from a few authentic clippings can add flavor to the presentation.

Here is an example of this method:

Red China

I have been asked to give you tonight the benefit of my observations about the international situation.

I was reading a very interesting news report the other day about Red China. The Chinese have been busy trying to get modern. They have had various programs like the old Russian Five Year Plan so they would move them ahead. They are sure that with communist methods they can surpass everyone else.

It seems that an American reporter got permission to visit Peking and was taken by a Chinese official to see the subway they have built there. First the official showed him the fine waiting rooms with bright lights and ample benches. Then he showed him the ticket booths and gleaming turnstiles. Then he showed him the fine wide stairways. Next he proudly displayed the air ducts and ventilators.

After about half an hour of this, the American turned to the official and said:

"This is all very interesting, I'm sure, but we've been

117

down here for at least 30 minutes and I haven't seen a single train."

"There you go!" said the guide belligerently. "How about those race riots in Birmingham?"

East Germany

But the communists in China aren't the only ones who are having their troubles. I was reading the other day about some of the difficulties the East German communists are having in patrolling the border with West Germany.

According to this story, a blank looking West German bicycled up to an East German customs station at the border. A huge burlap bag was fastened behind his bicycle seat.

"What's in it?" snapped the burly customs inspector.

"Straw," answered the West German.

"Straw!" barked the inspector. "Give me that sack!"

He angrily searched through the contents, feeling carefully through the straw inside but finding nothing. In frustration he searched the West German too but again with no success.

A week later the same thing happened all over again. The inspector was angrier than ever. He dumped the straw on the ground and searched through it in a frenzy. He checked the bag for secret pockets. He made the cyclist take off his shoes so he could look for hidden compartments in the heels. But he couldn't find a thing.

For months this went on. The inspector was beside himself—but still he found nothing.

Finally he could stand it no longer.

"Look," he said, as the cyclist rode up, "I'm not going to search you. I'm not going to question you. I just can't stand it any longer. I'll make a deal with you. I promise I won't stop you again or ask any questions if you will just *please* tell me what you've been smuggling in all this time."

"OK," said the West German, still expressionless. "A deal's a deal—— Bicycles."

Monaco

Our dedicated members of Congress make the sacrifice of going on many trips to all these foreign countries to see the problems first hand so that they can propose solutions. There seem to be a particularly large number of foreign crises facing us at the present time in the French Riviera. I keep reading that a number of our Congressmen are going to the trouble of journeying there. It may be that Monaco is planning to invade France. Of course, I don't believe the Princess there would start an invasion without advance warning. I'm sure she would allow a Grace period.

United States

Adam Clayton Powell is one of our fine Congressmen who manages to find time in his busy schedule for these vital trips to foreign lands. But I understand he is planning to divorce his wife. She served him Junket for dessert.

Governor George Wallace is reportedly divorcing his wife too. She gave him a colored television set for his birthday.

The Congo

Down in the Congo there has been so much commotion it has been hard for the beasts of the jungle to pursue a normal existence or even to get enough to eat.

Two tigers became so desperate that they walked right into Stanleyville one night and down the main street. As they passed a local drinking establishment they saw a typical barroom scene: a dressed up floozy standing at the bar trying to make time with a couple of male customers. Unable to control his hunger one of the tigers bounded into the bar and devoured the female.

The next day as the two tigers were walking through the jungle the daring one said to his companion:

"I don't know what's wrong with me today. I'm so drowsy I can hardly keep my eyes open."

"No wonder," said the other, "it's that bar-bitch-you-ate."

United Nations

When things were getting out of hand in the Congo the United Nations asked for volunteers to go down there and keep the peace. A large plane load assembled in New York made up of men from all different parts of the world. When the plane got half way across the ocean one of the four engines developed trouble. The pilot assured the assorted passengers they could make it on three engines but he had no sooner done so than a second engine went out.

The plane began to lose altitude and the pilot came on the public address system again and gave orders that all the seat cushions and baggage and everything with weight should be thrown overboard. But the plane continued to lose altitude. The pilot came on the PA and said:

"You are all brave patriotic men from your various countries. We can't stay in the air with everyone on board and there is a rough sea below so we can't ditch. We need some of you to volunteer to jump overboard."

There was a grim pause while the passengers looked around at each other. Finally two Englishmen got up from their seats, went to the open door, yelled "God Save the Queen" and jumped overboard.

After another pause two Frenchmen walked to the rear, yelled "Vive la France" and jumped.

Then there were two Germans who shouted "Deutschland Über Alles" before leaping out.

But the plane continued to lose altitude.

Finally two tall Texans stood up with grim looks on their faces, shouted "Remember the Alamo"—and threw two Mexicans overboard.

Peace Corps

You have no doubt all been following with interest the success of the Peace Corps in various parts of the world. I was interested in hearing about the recent visit of Sargent Shriver, the Peace Corps Director, to a cannibal island in the South Pacific. He flew in to check on a remote area far back in the jungles. When he made his way there he was greeted by the cannibal chief. The chief greeted him by saying:

"Mr. Shriver, your Peace Corps has done much for us. And the thing we appreciate the most of all is your wonderful Peace Corps Cookbook."

"Cookbook?" said Shriver, puzzled.

"Yes," said the chief. "Here," and he displayed a worn copy of a Peace Corp recruiting manual entitled "One Hundred Ways to Serve Your Fellow Man."

There is another Peace Corps incident that happened back in the jungles of one of the undeveloped African countries. There was a tribal king who lived in a big thatched-roof house in the center of the village. The king loved to do all kinds of ceremonial dances. He had a big high official chair right in the center of the floor of his thatched house and one day when he was stomping around doing a dance he ran into the chair and broke a toe.

One of the Peace Corpsmen who was assigned to the village did some first aid and then he suggested that when the king wanted to dance he should put the official chair up in the rafters of the house out of the way. When the king's toe healed up, he followed the Peace Corpsman's suggestion and put the official chair up out of the way. But then a few days later when he was doing a particularly violent dance and causing a lot of vibration, the official chair jarred loose and fell down on the king's head.

Which all goes to show that people who live in grass houses shouldn't stow thrones.

De Gaulle

Many of our international problems are due to General De Gaulle. He is so uncooperative and headstrong. You probably heard that the French are considering buying the Rock of Gibraltar from the British and renaming it De Gaulle Stone.

But General De Gaulle isn't as young as he used to be. Only recently he sent one of his most trusted lieutenants out to look for an appropriate burial spot. The assistant spent several weeks looking and came back to report he had found the perfect spot: a pleasant, secluded hillside out in the countryside overlooking the Seine.

But the General was not pleased. He told his aide he did not want to be buried in a secluded spot but in some location where there were graves of other very important people.

The aide was gone again for two weeks but this time he came back and reported that with great difficulty he had arranged to purchase the very last remaining plot in the most exclusive, most historic, and most expensive cemetery in France.

De Gaulle was pleased.

"How much will it cost?" he asked.

"Two hundred thousand francs," said the aide.

De Gaulle looked troubled.

"That's a terribly high price to pay," he said, "for only three days."

Making Stories Topical

Many stories can be given a topical flavor by tying them to items currently in the news. For instance:

Smith commented to his friend Jones how well Jones and his wife got along and asked Jones for the secret of their happy marriage.

"It's very easy. We agreed the day we were married that we would avoid all cause for argument. I agreed that she could have the last word on all minor questions and she agreed I would have the last word on all the major ones."

"That's terrific. But how do you know which category a question fits in? What kind of things are minor, for instance?"

"Oh, such things as where I'll work, where we'll live, where we'll go on our vacation, where our children will go to college, things like that." Smith was astonished.

"*Those* are *minor* questions! Then what are some major ones?"

"Well, for example, whether we should get out of Vietnam, whether we should give De Gaulle our nuclear secrets, whether we should recognize Red China. Things like that!"

XVI

Speeches Before Small Groups

Not all speeches are in auditoriums and banquet halls with podiums and microphones.

Many are in small informal groups—in living rooms, board rooms, classrooms, and sales rooms. The smaller the room the closer the speaker is to his audience, not just physically, but psychologically.

It is bad enough to pontificate before a large audience, with no sparkle and no humor. But a large event is more likely to be stiff and formal, and the audience there is not too surprised to be subjected to a stuffy speaker. But stiffness and stuffiness

125

can be fatal before a small group in a small room. Excessive formality and pomp are, under those circumstances, so out of place as to be ludicrous.

Don't Do This

I remember a meeting of the fathers of students at the grade school my daughter Jerry was attending in Short Hills, New Jersey. The principal had asked the fathers to come on a designated evening but had not explained why. A crowd of busy men assembled in a classroom and were rather surprised to find that the purpose of the gathering was to discuss forming an all male PTA to supplement the existing all female PTA.

To my amazement there were a number of speeches —often several by the same man—discussing this ridiculous suggestion in an ultraserious vein. I recall particularly one father who made a stirring address drawing an analogy to the Monroe Doctrine! (Presumably the mother PTA leaders were keeping the fathers out as the United States is supposed to keep foreign powers out of Latin American nations.)

The discussion became focused on whether the proposed organization (the meetings of which I am sure none of those present planned to attend) should be formal and independent or whether it should be a loose, informal auxiliary of the existing PTA. After the argument about formal versus informal had waxed and waned for an unbelievable hour or so, a prominent doctor sitting next to me brought the whole business to an end by getting the floor and stating:

"I wonder if I could summarize the results of this

meeting by saying we have agreed to form the loose Fathers club of Short Hills."

It was a fitting conclusion for a very unnecessary meeting.

However, let us assume that it was really important to sell this idea rather than have it subjected to pompous pontification and to ridicule. With some charm and finesse and a little touch of humor this proposal might have been put over.

Do This

Here is the way it might have been introduced:

Good evening, gentlemen. I know you are curious as to why we asked you to come here tonight instead of watching the wrestling matches on television. We want to get your ideas about the PTA.

Now don't let that frighten you. Don't be like a lady I know who didn't feel well and went to see her doctor. He examined her and announced that she was normal in every respect except that she was pregnant.

> The lady gasped in deep distress:
> "Oh, I can't stand it!"
> "But madame, you have had three children before," said the doctor. "That was some years ago, I realize. But you didn't have any particular difficulty before, did you?"
> "No. But I can't bear to face it."
> "To face *what*?"
> "Going through that PTA again!"

We aren't suggesting that you busy gentlemen should be active on a week-by-week or month-by-month basis in

PTA activities. We aren't suggesting that the fathers become rivals of the mothers in having a PTA organization. We aren't proposing that you sell cookies or hold rummage sales.

The existing PTA does all that. But what they lack is hard headed experienced advice on their policy and business matters. For example, there has been a proposal that the PTA should have a fund raising drive to pay for landscaping the front of the school grounds. But the fine ladies, your wives, don't even know if that would be legal. They don't know what they would be getting into in the way of cost and obligation. They need guidance. They need advice on program.

I know some of you feel you are already doing enough for this school with all the taxes you pay. I know others feel they already hear enough about these problems. Back when Winston Churchill was Prime Minister of England one of his cabinet ministers approached him with great excitement and said:

> "Winston, have I told you about my new grandchild?"
> "No," said Churchill, "and you don't know how much I appreciate it."

Well we won't be boring you with a lot of things you don't have time to hear about. We would meet about once every three months. I think it's a sensible and workable idea. I think it will make for a better school. What do some of the rest of you think?

Let Audience Participate

Too often people making presentations to small, informal groups try to cover every conceivable detail in their initial statement. They feel that if one of the hearers later asks a pertinent question it indicates that the person making the opening statement did not do a complete job and has been caught short. But informal sessions are much more effective if some of the key points are brought out by answers to questions. It gives the listeners that all important sense of participation. If they think they were the first ones to whom the question occurred it flatters their egos and may help to get them committed to whatever is being discussed.

The phrase "I'm glad you asked that question, Senator" has a humorous twist, but there is a great deal of value in being able to use a question as an excuse for supplementing the initial pitch and to buttress the argument. If the right questions are never asked, the key points they would have introduced can be covered in a further statement or wind up summary.

A Brief Speech for a
Small Group

There is a different kind of situation involving a small group which is illustrated by this story:

At a speaking event where a large crowd was expected only a handful of people showed up. The scheduled speaker asked the program chairman if he thought they should go ahead with the speech. The chairman, a wise old bird, answered:

"When I used to work down on the farm, if I took the trouble to haul a load of feed to the barn lot and unexpectedly only one or two cows showed up instead of 100, I fed the one or two anyway."

Reassured, the speaker stood up and delivered his

prepared speech which was an hour long. When he finished and sat down he turned to the chairman and said brightly:

"How was it?"

"Terrible. Much too long."

"But you told me that if only one or two cows showed up you fed them anyway."

"Sure. But I didn't say I gave them the whole load!"

Talking too long is the single biggest defect in speeches both of the formal and informal variety.

I have never heard a speech criticized on the ground that it was too short.

Brevity Indicates Preparation

The long speech often results from failure of the speaker to properly organize his thoughts. This indicates carelessness, lack of preparation, and inadequate time devoted to weeding out repetition, extraneous material, and unclear statements which require elaboration and explanation.

Lincoln once ended up a long letter with this statement:

"I am sorry I am so rushed I didn't have time to make this short."

Another common defect of talks to small groups is that the speaker, in a misconceived effort to seem informal and conversational, fails to speak up and can't be heard. Never mumble or mutter to a few of those nearby in the mistaken belief that this evidences commendable humility and deference. Talk to the person furthest away from you, so that no one will think a private little group is conspiring in semisecrecy.

Have a Moderator

No matter how small or informal the group, someone should be in charge or should take charge. The "after you, Gaston" approach to getting a meeting started or explaining what it is about leads to wasted time for everyone. If there is doubt as to which of two or three people is going to run the meeting it should be straightened out among them in advance and not by a process of public jockeying for position.

"Frank, you call the meeting to order, introduce Fred and Carl and me and Dr. Turmions, and read the agenda for the meeting. The rest of us will pitch in when you get to the subject of moving the national headquarters to Chicago, but you keep the discussion confined to the subject before us and we won't try to interfere. Don't be too diffident about those who try to wander into other problems and don't worry about us thinking you are trying to take over. We can take turns on this at other meetings, but the important thing is to avoid all those time-wasting harangues about trifles that we had at our session last month."

Organize

For a small meeting be sure to have a written agenda and read it off in advance. That in itself tends to separate the mountains from the mole hills.

I once was on a church board where at the first meeting I attended the substantial men present spent over an hour debating the question of whether the church, a very wealthy one, should pay for mowing the assistant minister's lawn. Anyone of those present could have earned enough in that hour to pay for mowing the lawn all summer. I decided that board wasn't for me.

One time I was asked to attend a meeting of a business organization called on short notice to discuss a supposedly important topic. About 15 high-level executives attended. It turned out the question before the house was why so few employees had attended the employees' dance. It was incredible the way those 15 busy administrators managed to worry that subject for a solid hour.

Announce Agenda

By announcing the agenda in advance the chairman encourages those present to give short shrift to the minor items and to conserve the time for the important ones. The agenda may be:

1. Place of the next meeting.
2. Paying the traveling expenses of the executive secretary to attend an out of town seminar.
3. Buying new furniture for the director's room.
4. Moving the headquarters to Richmond.

If the agenda is not announced in advance, 95 per cent of the total time may be spent in talk about the first three items. Then the important item, number four, may have to be disposed of in an offhand manner with inadequate discussion. Or the meeting may run heavily over the scheduled time. Some of those present may have left for other engagements without realizing that the genuinely vital agenda item was being held to the last.

To see why this is so, we must remember one of Professor Parkinson's most important parables. A board of directors met to consider two subjects: 1. Whether the company should spend $1,500 to enlarge the employees' bicycle shed, and 2. whether $25 million should be spent to finance a new atomic power plant. The discussion of the power plant took about one minute because no one considered himself sufficiently expert to have an opinion about an atomic installation. But everyone was sure he knew as much or more than the others about what a bicycle shed should cost and the argument over that item continued for two hours with a decision to postpone it for further discussion at the next meeting.

Someone has to be in charge and has to pace the agenda in accordance with the priorities, to avoid having all the time devoted to the inconsequential. Everyone can understand and have an opinion on the inconsequential.

If the chairman of the Short Hills fathers' meeting had given the discussion direction and had lined up in advance a couple of men who would speak in support of the idea, he could have gotten someplace.

Too often those who might logically take charge fear appearing to be overaggressive. But people would rather see the necessary business disposed of in an orderly fashion and the meeting over on time. The secret is to be not just a boss, but a nice boss.

XVII

Old Jokes—Pro and Con

Some jokes are so old and well worn that they acquire a new status as a standard joke. A reference to such a joke provides a short cut method of expressing an idea.

For example, a speaker might say that he had written to a company complaining about poor service and the company replied by sending him a "bedbug letter."

This refers, of course, to a familiar, true-to-life story.

A traveler on a Pullman car woke up in the morning and found that during the night he had acquired several bedbug bites. When he arrived at his office he promptly dispatched an angry and anguished letter of complaint to the president of the Pullman company. In the course of time he received a letter from the assistant vice president of the company as follows:

> Our president has asked me to reply to your letter about your most unfortunate experience on a Pullman car on the night of September 17. He was greatly disturbed to receive your complaint and ordered an immediate exhaustive investigation headed by a high-level task force of company officials. Never before have we received even a hint of a situation such as your report. Despite the fact that in our 70 years of service our company has never before been faced with such an appalling incident, we are determined to leave no stone unturned to avoid a recurrence at all costs. We apologize profusely and thank you for calling this unprecedented matter to our attention.

Unfortunately the secretary in mailing out this letter had left clipped to it the original complaint letter from the passenger to the president. And scrawled on the original, over the president's initials were these words: "Send this jerk the bedbug letter."

Allusions

In speeches and conversation one customarily makes allusions to incidents in Scripture or Shakespeare or even in popular songs or comic strips. We say: "I don't want to walk into the lion's den," or "He's sort of a Shylock," or "She hides her age nearly as well as Orphan Annie." Familiar jokes provide the same kind of convenient, descriptive references:

The "what-have-you-done-for-me-lately" attitude to-

ward public office holders. This refers to the classic Alben Barkley story about the voter who was not going to vote for reelection of the Congressman who had gotten 1. the voter's brother a job, 2. his father an increase in his pension, and 3. his company a government contract.

The Will Rogers definition of the Democratic party: I don't belong to any organized political party— I'm a Democrat.

Decisions, decisions, decisions, referring to the reason given by a woman quitting her job in a cannery where she separated the ripe tomatoes from the green ones.

Beware of Current Jokes

The jokes to be wary of are not so much those that have been around a long time, as those that are circulating actively in current vogue. When a joke is "going around" at the moment at high velocity, chances are that many other people have heard it and—worst of all— heard it recently.

This is particularly true of short, topical jokes.

During the 1964 Presidential campaign all kinds of people were busy passing along this one.

> Goldwater was asked in a TV interview what would be the first thing he would do if he were President in the event of imminent threat of a missile attack on our country.
> "The very first thing I would do," he supposedly says, "is to order that all the wagons be drawn up into a circle."

One new joke about Johnson was told to me three times in a single day by a lawyer at my office in Washington, in the course of a telephone call from a client in

Chicago, and in a PS to a business letter from Los Angeles.

Wide Selection Available

But very few jokes become completely worn out and very few become Standard Jokes. Many jokes that go over best in speeches are not really new but they are highly usable because they never circulated very actively or because they have been brought up-to-date by using current names and situations.

Some jokes are too subtle or specialized to circulate widely. Or they may be somewhat hard to tell because they involve use of an accent or require a particularly good memory. Not everyone can use an Italian accent. Not everyone can keep tongue and mind closely enough in gear to quote the drunk:

"You may think I've had tee many martoonis, but I'm not so much under the affluence of incohol as some thinkle peep."

In addition, as I mentioned elsewhere, most people don't remember jokes. If some time elapses after they have heard one, they may vaguely recall that they heard it before, but if it is funny they will like it again.

One minor tragedy which comes from using humor in speeches (and I have seen this happen more than once) is for a speaker to tell a story which, unknown to him, a previous speaker told the same audience at an earlier session of the same gathering. I don't know any practicable way to insure against this except, as I say, to be wary of current jokes that are "going around" at high velocity.

A speaker arriving to speak on the last day of a three-day convention can't very well quiz the program chairman as to every joke that might have been told by a previous speaker. If he has a prepared, canned joke and is not going to select one off the cuff at the last minute he can, of course, ask the program chairman: "Did anyone else tell this story that is going around about the newly-weds in the Volkswagen?" But the speaker probably has more important things to think about at that point and I don't suggest that he add such an inquiry to his pre-speech "check list."

The Old Reliable Joke

Some jokes and humorous remarks that always bring a laugh actually have long and distinguished histories. Many a Congressman will say:

"I hate patronage. Whenever I succeed in getting someone appointed to a much sought-after federal job I end up making ten enemies and one ingrate."

Abraham Lincoln used that remark and I used to think it originated with him. But recently I discovered that some researcher had dug up the fact that an almost identical statement was made over 250 years ago by Louis XIV.

There is a good political story which can be used successfully, switching the party labels, at a political meeting involving either side:

Jones asked Brown:
"Why on earth are you a Democrat?"
"Because my father was a Democrat and my grandfather was a Democrat."
"What a stupid, weak-kneed reason. Why don't you

make your own decisions? What if your father had been a horse thief and your grandfather had been a bank robber?" "Why then I'd be a Republican."

Apparently this story was first used by Theodore Roosevelt—with the party names the other way around of course. Maybe it was told long before his time. But most people haven't heard it.

Our forebears were not always so stiff and serious as we might think. Many of them told wonderful jokes that have been generally forgotten and are highly usable today.

My 96-year-old father, who retains his excellent memory, once told me that he could remember hearing 50 years ago a joke I told him. It was new to me and my contemporaries.

How Do Jokes Circulate?

Reportedly a great deal of the uncanny speed with which a good joke moves from coast to coast results from stories being sent in slack moments over stock-brokers' teletypes and direct wires. These specialists are communicating avidly all day and there is some free time available for "have you heard this one?"

Here's another example of a Standard Joke that has been circulated so widely that the punch line, used alone, has become an expressive catch phrase.

Sam Brown and Liza Wells were celebrating the fourth birthday of their son and they decided it was about time they got married. They climbed in the old wagon and journeyed to the county seat, located the judge and asked him to marry them.

They apparently knew nothing about the need for a

marriage license so the judge sent them down to the county clerk on the next floor of the court house to get a license. In due course, they came back with a license authorizing him to marry Sam Brown and Liza Wells. After inspecting it, he turned to Sam and said, "Sam Brown? Say, your name is Samuel, isn't it?" Sam replied, "Judge, that's right but everybody calls me Sam." The judge instructed them to go right back to the clerk's office and get the license made out in the name of Samuel Brown. When they returned, he took another look at it and inquired of Liza if her real name shouldn't be shown as Elizabeth. When she admitted that it should, he again sent them back to the clerk's office. Finally they returned, the judge looked over the license and said, "Your license is in order now and I have no choice but to marry you. But, I want you clearly to understand, that boy of yours will remain a technical bastard." To this Sam replied, with a smile on his face, "Judge, that ain't so bad. That's what the clerk said you are."

A less familiar story along the same line concerns a small town merchant who by scrimping and saving was able to give a top flight education to each of his three sons, one as a doctor, one as a lawyer, and one as an engineer. One Christmas when the sons were visiting their parents the father said that he and their mother were worn out from working so long and so hard and were considering buying their first car and taking a vacation trip if the sons would lend them a little money.

The doctor spoke up and explained that he had no extra funds because of the expense of his new house, and the payments on his new boat. The lawyer had the same story: he had been furnishing a new office and sending his

140

children to expensive camps. The engineer likewise said he was broke from paying so much income tax and buying a new ranch.

"Well," said the father, "I'm sorry we can't make the trip. It's not myself I care about. It's your mother. I feel I owe her something. I've never told you this before but do you know we have both had our noses to the grindstone so constantly we have never even had time to go and get a marriage license and have a ceremony performed."

"Father," said all three sons in unison. "Do you realize what that makes *us?*"

"Yes," said the father, "and cheap ones, too."

Don't Kid Yourself about a Joke

One of the oddest joke-telling incidents I ever observed was at a fancy dinner party in a private home in Short Hills, New Jersey. One of the guests, a highly successful business executive, became carried away with his belief (mistaken) that he was an accomplished story teller. He rose from the table and regaled the diners from the sidelines by telling—as though it was his own private true story—one of the best-known Standard Jokes there is.

I could hardly believe my ears as this gentleman, supposedly describing one of his Negro employees, told about the man who came home unexpectedly when his wife was upstairs with another man. The executive reported gleefully, in the lines which he didn't seem to realize were familiar to all present, how the wife called down:

"Who dat?"

The husband said nothing.

Again the wife called, "Who dat?"

Again the husband was silent.

The third time the "other man" called down, "Who dat?"

At this point I broke in on the performing business-man with:

"Who dat say dat last *who dat?*"

The executive was flabbergasted. He wanted to know where I had heard this private story of his about what had happened to *his* employee. I have never known to this day whether he really did think this was his own personal, private anecdote. Maybe the incident actually did happen to the man who worked for him and became the original source of the familiar story.

There are lots of theories as to who "makes up" funny stories. I have heard, though I am inclined to doubt it, that many of the smutty ones originate in prisons.

There is a Standard Joke about the new prisoner who was baffled, his first night at the supper table, to hear another inmate say "83," at which all the others at the table laughed; another said "56" and everyone roared. Later the new prisoner asked his cellmate what it was all about. The cellmate replied:

"We know all of each other's jokes by heart from hearing them dozens of times. So we have given each joke a number."

The next night the new prisoner waited for a strategic moment and said brightly "71." There was dead silence. After a pause he ventured "37," again no response.

Later he asked his cellmate what was wrong.

The cellmate shrugged:

"Don't feel bad. Some people just don't know how to tell a joke."

XVIII

Sources of Material

The best source of humor for
speeches is back numbers of the
Reader's Digest.

The *Digest* is on the whole a
rather evangelical magazine telling
us how to stop worrying, how to stop
smoking, how to stop overeating. In
fact, it is not a magazine for the person who feels that everything he
enjoys is either illegal, immoral, or
fattening. Reading the *Digest* is a little like they used to say about being a
Presbyterian: it doesn't keep you
from sinning, it just keeps you from
enjoying it.

But the magazine really does a

good job of assembling and publishing humor, and even breaking it down into categories. And it pays worthwhile money for contributions. One hundred dollars is paid for contributions to "Life in these United States" (true stories revealing *adult* human nature) and to "Humor in Uniform"; $25 or more is paid for items accepted for such categories as "Laughter, the Best Medicine."

(Let me pause here to congratulate the editors for sticking to *adult* human nature. Much as I admire Art Linkletter as a fine gentleman, I am strictly allergic to a heavy diet of "bright sayings of children.")

"Reader's Digest" as Source

Years ago the *Digest* carried a story which is an example of my statement elsewhere that most really funny jokes can be used successfully even if they are old because few will remember them even if they once heard them.

> Several ladies at a card party were discussing prenatal influence. One said:
> "It's really uncanny. Shortly before I was born my mother burned herself while lighting a stove and I've been terribly afraid of fire all my life."
> "I'm the same way," another said. "A few weeks before I came into the world my mother fell off a footbridge and nearly drowned and I've always been terribly afraid of water."
> A third lady spoke up scoffingly.
> "That's all nonsense. There's nothing to that silly theory. Before I was born my mother was carrying a stack of phonograph records and fell down and cracked every one of them. But it didn't affect me . . . affect me . . . affect me."

As an example of how many jokes are adaptations of earlier versions, here is a story of much later vintage which is "out of the same card file."

A nervous man was taking his first airplane trip. After surviving the take off he was trying to relax when a voice came over the public address system:

"Good afternoon, ladies and gentlemen. Welcome aboard. You will be interested to know that you are participating in the very first 100 per cent automated airplane flight. There is no one in the pilot's cabin. All the controls are completely automatic and electronic. The voice you hear is a recording. But you have absolutely nothing to fear. This sensational mechanized system has been completely tested and checked out before this flight. There is no chance whatever of anything going wrong anywhere in this coordinated system. It is absolutely foolproof . . . absolutely foolproof . . . absolutely foolproof."

Avoid Current Issues

Obviously I do not suggest that a speaker should use a joke from the current issue of *Reader's Digest* or even from an issue of a few months back. I did that once, not having read the current month's offerings and therefore not realizing where the story came from. Several people told me afterward that they had seen the story too! But if it had been in a one- or two-year-old issue few would have remembered.

There are numerous books of jokes and anecdotes. For some reason I don't have much luck in finding anything I want in them. But they can be found under classification 808 in any public library and perhaps may contain just what a particular speaker is looking for.

Lincolnesque Humor

I myself am a great fan of Abraham Lincoln humor, and I find audiences generally enjoy stories from that distinguished source. Many of the best of Lincoln's humorous statements have been assembled in a book entitled *The Lincoln Treasury*, compiled by Caroline Thomas Harnsberger and published by Wilcox and Follett Co.

Carl Sandburg in Volume II of *War Years* quotes this parable told by Lincoln when, as usual, he was being besieged by office seekers:

> One time, minding a mud scow in a bayou near the Yazoo, [I] read a story of a certain king who called the Court Minister, said he wanted to go hunting, and asked the Minister if it would rain. The Minister told him the weather would be fair, it would not rain, and he could go hunting. The royal party on the way met a farmer riding a jackass. He told the king to turn back, it was going to rain. The king laughed, went on, and no sooner got started hunting than a heavy downpour of rain drenched him and his party to their royal skins. The king went back to the palace, threw out the Minister, and called for the farmer.
>
> "Tell me how you knew it would rain."
>
> "I did not know, Your Majesty, it's not me, it's my jackass. He puts his ears forward when it's going to be wet and back when it's going to be dry weather."
>
> The king sent the farmer away, had the jackass brought and put in the place of the Minister.
>
> It was here . . . the king made a great mistake . . . [because] ever since that time, every jackass wants an office . . .

During Lincoln's time there was no such thing as Civil Service, which explains the endless harassment he suffered from job seekers on top of all his worries about the Civil War.

During his trip to Gettysburg to make his famous address, Lincoln contracted a serious contagious fever. But when he came back the job seekers descended on him anyway. In that day all kinds of people entered the White House unbidden and sought the President's attention even while he was walking about in his own premises. Lincoln's secretary sought to keep the jobseekers out of the bedroom where Lincoln lay ill but Lincoln said:

"Let them all come in. At last I have something I can give everybody."

Perhaps I like such Lincoln stories because they reveal so pointedly that, unlike the usual politician, he dared to call a spade a spade. I also like these vivid reminders that "being funny" is not an obstacle to becoming President or to being a great man, despite what some people said about Adlai Stevenson during his campaigns. Stevenson just had the bad luck to run against an incredibly popular personality. Lincoln had strong opposition too when he ran in 1860, but it was divided between two other candidates, and he won with only 40 per cent of the popular vote.

Eisenhower enjoyed hearing humorous stories at private gatherings but he didn't attempt to use humor in public. Kennedy used dry, quick quips and cracks—often sharp and even derisive. He rarely used "that reminds me" stories. Lyndon Johnson on the other hand uses stories, usually of a folksy nature, at the beginning of a prepared speech, and often uses the same story many times.

Politicians Good Source of Humor

The remarks of politicians and public figures are very frequently good sources of humor and the appeal to the audience is increased because a well-known man is named as the source.

During his administration Franklin Roosevelt took some controversial action which particularly infuriated "Cotton Ed" Smith, an anti-New Deal Senator from South Carolina. A friend, in trying to mollify Cotton Ed, said:

"Roosevelt is his own worst enemy."

At which Smith spluttered:

"Not while *I'm* alive."

Similarly, when Churchill was Prime Minister, a friend tried to find something nice to say about a leader of the opposition.

"Hes' a very modest man."

"He has a great deal to be modest about," snapped Churchill.

Orville Freeman, the dynamic and personable Secretary of Agriculture, was addressing a large banquet crowd:

"It's a pleasure to be here with such a distinguished audience. I am particularly glad to see that so many of the ladies have come. After all, behind every successful man is . . . a surprised mother-in-law."

The Appendix to the daily Congressional Record is an excellent source of speech ideas and source material. Editorials, speeches, columns, and comments are reprinted here verbatim. Some of them include humorous introductory material.

Occasionally a speech in the Congressional Record reminds us that there are world-shaking problems we may never even have heard about that should be causing us intense worry.

For example, here is a statement in the Record by the distinguished junior Senator from Montana:

MR. METCALF: Mr. President, I call attention to a very serious situation that has developed in my State.

I have been advised, by a legal firm in my home town of Helena, that one of its clients, a rancher, is unable to obtain a competent horsebreaker or trainer.

The rancher has been in touch with an Australian with impressive qualifications, who seeks to enter this country to engage in the storied profession of "bronc peeling."

Under the rules of the Immigration Department, in order for the Australian to enter this country there must be a certification by the Labor Department that there is not an American supply of horse trainers who are unemployed.

The Department of Labor did indeed certify that "qualified workers are not available within the United States for referral to the employer by the Employment Service."

Mr. President, what will the American image be abroad if it becomes known that the Nation of cowboys and Indians, which exports hundreds of western movies, where even former Presidents read western novels, has to import a horse wrangler from the other side of the world?

I certainly will not stand in the way of any Australian who seeks to come to our shores to follow his profession. But I wish to let my colleagues know that employment opportunities, for which some of their constituents may possibly qualify, do exist in my State.

The shortage of competent wranglers in Montana —the land of the Great Greenoughs, Lindermans, and Reynolds—derives from the fact that Montana wranglers are busy picking up top money in rodeos in other states.

Keep a File

I cannot emphasize too strongly the advisability of jotting down and keeping a file of jokes and stories one hears. If the listener likes the story himself chances are he will be able to tell it with enthusiasm. The important thing is to write down enough of the story so that it can be recalled accurately without losing the flavor of it.

For a very important event an inexperienced speaker should not be afraid to employ a ghost-writer. This is done, for example, by the principal speakers at the big Gridiron Dinners given each spring in Washington. It is a highly critical audience and the speakers are supposed to be funny and original. The use of professional writers is entirely in order.

Even in a moderate-sized community chances are there is some member of the working press who is good at putting together a humorous text. If the speaker is inexperienced and the occasion is important to him, he should employ such assistance.

XIX

Commencement Speeches

A commencement speech is far different in its approach and content than an afterdinner speech. But it does not need to be merely an outpouring of pomposity. It should have some brightness and lightness.

The purpose should be to provide something interesting for the graduates themselves. Instead, commencement speakers too often use the occasion to produce material for a printed text which they can circulate, with their business card attached, to an extensive personal mailing list. And it does not matter to this type of speaker whether or not the text is really appropriate for an audience of graduates and their parents.

"The Threat of the Dual Distribution System to Our Free Markets" may enable the speaker to expound on a pet subject, but what does it have to do with finishing the four-year course at Upper Peabody U.?

Be Brief

Yale University does not have an outside commencement speaker, but they make a big thing of the baccalaureate service. The story goes that an Episcopal Bishop appeared to make the baccalaureate sermon. He announced that his remarks would be built upon those four wonderful letters Y—A—L—E.

"Y," he said, "stands for youth." And with great vigor he talked for 15 minutes on youth.

"A is for ambition." And he became more ambitious and talked for 20 minutes on ambition.

"L is for loyalty." That took 25 minutes to cover.

"Finally, E stands for enthusiasm."

With that the Bishop became so enthusiastic he talked for 40 minutes on enthusiasm.

As the Bishop came down the aisle after the sermon he noticed one of the graduates with his head in his hand in an attitude of prayer.

"Young man," said the Bishop stopping, "I see that something I said has had a profound effect on you. I wonder if you would tell me what particular point impressed you so much."

"Well, Bishop. It's this way. I was just sitting here giving thanks I didn't go to the Massachusetts Institute of Technology."

Don't Be Stuffy

In 1962 when I was Postmaster General I was invited to make the commencement address at Illinois College in Jacksonville, Illinois, the city where I was born 47 years previously. It was a beautifully run occasion and I used some introductory paragraphs which were intended not only to demonstrate to the graduates that I was not a stuffed shirt, but also to identify myself with the location.

Two score and seven years ago my father brought forth into this city a new baby—conceived and dedicated to the proposition that all men should have good mail service.

I do not mean to underplay my mother's participation in this event, but my father played a dual role in the undertaking, not only as parent but as attending physician.

At the time I was born, my father owned a private surgical hospital here in Jacksonville. My mother had little choice as to who would be her physician—but she didn't have to pay a doctor's bill either. I suppose it was an early example of what the American Medical Association would call "socialized medicine."

Jacksonville has many significant ties for me. For one thing, it was named after Andrew Jackson.

Jackson had many distinctions.

He fought and won the great Battle of New Orleans because he didn't know the War of 1812 was already over. He thus is the most illustrious case in government history of a man who "didn't get the word."

But one of Democrat Andrew Jackson's overlooked distinctions is that he appointed Abraham Lincoln a *postmaster*—of New Salem, Illinois—not far from here.

It was Lincoln's first public job.

My family moved away from Jacksonville, to Springfield, when I was three years old.

My recollection of that event is hazy.

But I must have been a remarkable three-year-old. For since I have ended up in charge of 580,000 postal employees and 45,000 postal locations, any number of people who want jobs or want to build or equip post offices, write to remind me that they knew me *intimately* when I lived here in Jacksonville.

Some even say they were devoted friends of my sister.

The only trouble is I never had a sister.

But it is wonderful to know that I was so gregarious and widely respected at the age of three!

William Jennings Bryan not only graduated from your college, but he also began law practice in Jacksonville.

Stephen A. Douglas also started law practice here.

Since Adlai Stevenson came from Bloomington, Illinois, not far away, one can't help but note that downstate Illinois has produced an unusual number of distinguished but unsuccessful Democratic candidates for President of the United States.

One big fault with many commencement speeches is that they are cliché ridden:

"I stand here before you as you prepare to leave

155

the cloistered calm of academic halls and go out into the great world, etc."

Talk to Your Audience

College students and new college graduates do not consider themselves as innocent of the world around them as some commencement speakers seem to think. They do not like to be talked down to or lectured to or preached at. They will listen with much greater receptiveness if the speaker discusses with them some subject of current concern as though they were intelligent adults.

Another big fault is in exhorting graduates about some problem which most of them can't be expected to be able to do anything about. There is no use telling them that the educational system of which they are recent products is no good, unless many of them are going to be college presidents and deans. There is even less reason to tell them a lot of people are in college who have no business being there.

Don't Use Audience

On occasion a commencement speaker will use his address as a means of firing an additional shot in some running battle he is engaged in over a pet controversy. He will say:

> After my speech two months ago before the Michigan Chapter of the National Education Association, I received several angry letters from individuals who disagreed with my views on use of the quarter system in four-year colleges and universities. I could see from these letters, and from an editorial in the April issue of the Michigan Educator that my proposal was misunderstood—perhaps deliberately. Therefore, I want to take this opportunity before this intelligent and

reasonable and open-minded audience of new graduates to clear up the misconceptions about my much discussed recommendations.

Probably very few people but the speaker realized his suggestion was "much discussed." But he is "using" a captive commencement audience for his own selfish purpose rather than complimenting the graduates by talking about something of genuine interest to them.

Don't Be Artificial

It isn't necessary to include any side-splitting jokes in order to give a commencement speech a light touch. Some picturesque language and specific stories and examples are all that are needed to avoid the stilted, artificial oratory so often used in these presentations.

Here is the opening, and some typical paragraphs, from a charming commencement address at Syracuse University by Professor Gilbert Highet of Columbia University. It is entitled "The Pleasures of Learning."

The Chinese have a huge vocabulary of curses. Their maledictions cover almost every aspect of human life, and go into marvelous, microscopic detail. We in the West can scarcely hope to rival them. We can be forcible, but rarely inventive. We can be blunt, but scarcely subtle. One in particular of their curses is quite beyond us; and here it is. When a Chinese finds one of his enemies particularly obnoxious, he creates a truly horrible wish for his future. He says to him: "MAY YOU PASS YOUR LIFE IN INTERESTING TIMES!"

He means what you and I are finding out: that it is difficult and exhausting to live in a period which is historically full of activity. You and I—whether it is the result of a curse or simply of our own bad luck—live in interesting times.

* * *

May I offer some advice to enhance the enjoyment of learning?

The first and most obvious counsel is to choose a worthy subject. There was a Russian Grand Duke in Anatole France, who had all the money and power anyone could wish, but could think of nothing better to do than to collect match-book covers. From time to time in the motion pictures, one sees a short film devoted to Curious Occupations; and it is nearly always a sombre warning against wasting one's life. You will see a lady who collects abalone shells, and sorts them out until she finds those which look like Californian landscapes, and then carves them and paints them until they look still more like Californian landscapes. When she appears on the motion pictures, or Ed Sullivan's show, or wherever it is, she has spent 25 years making abalone shells into the semblance of Californian landscapes, and, judging by her face as she looks into the camera, she has begun to realize her mistake. That is the kind of mistake we must be careful to avoid.

* * *

Many people have exercised themselves to death. Many people have played themselves to death. Many people have eaten and drunk themselves to death. Many people worry themselves to death. No one has ever thought himself to death. Thought is the only human activity which does not generate harmful acids and painful alkalis.

Avoid Clichés

A commencement address should be the one, most important place to avoid the phoney clichés and stereotypes of canned oratory. The test by which they can be spotted and weeded out is to ask yourself if that is the way you would talk to a trio of friends at a luncheon table or a cocktail party or riding along in a car. *Would* you say:

"I cannot adequately express to you how delighted and honored I am by the privilege of being here with you today. In my 18 happy years here in Mudville I have not participated in an occasion which gave me so much pleasure."

Of course you wouldn't. Your friends would think you had gone out of your mind, or that you were pulling an elaborate joke.

Yet take a look at any half dozen prepared texts of commencement addresses and at least five of them will be loaded, to a revolting extent, with trite and tiresome bromides, unctuous flattery, stuffy posturing.

XX

The Master of Ceremonies

A toastmaster or presiding officer should always have a knowledgeable liaison man or woman close at hand. The liaison person in turn should know at any minute how to locate the banquet manager and the men in charge of waiters, microphone, and spotlights.

If, despite advance checking, the reading light on the podium will not work, the presiding officer should not have to 1. scramble under the table looking for an electric outlet, 2. leave the speakers' table to look for assistance, or—worst of all—3. announce over the microphone that the electrician is wanted immediately.

Too often at the luncheon or banquet of a charity or a trade association the paid staff is eager to relax in dignity at the head table instead of fulfilling the essential but unglamorous function of glorified errand boy and liaison man for the presiding officer.

A good example of what I am warning against was furnished by a big black tie banquet I attended at the Statler-Hilton Hotel in Washington. The program showed that there were to be 12 people seated at the main speakers' table and others at a less important head table behind it.

Have Exact, Complete Arrangements

After a reception lasting an hour and a half in an adjoining room the audience poured into the banquet hall. When nearly everyone was seated it was discovered at the last minute that the front speakers' table had only eight places. As a result a retired Supreme Court justice, his wife, and an important United States Senator were left with no place to sit.

The others at the head table were equally important so they could not very well be ousted. There was no way to enlarge the inadequate head table because it was crowded onto a raised platform which was hemmed in by other crowded tables. It was an embarrassing mess. In the end the retired justice and his wife had to be seated at another table.

Someone should have double-checked this important

detail during the reception and before the crowd came into the banquet hall.

On another occasion I was acting as Master of Ceremonies for a big fund raising barbecue for Senator Gail McGee of Wyoming. It was held on the extensive grounds of the home of Sargent Shriver near Rockville, Maryland. The main dish was genuine buffalo meat and it gave me an opportunity for plenty of preliminary comments:

"As the old song goes—'Give me a home where the buffalo roam'—and I'll show you a dirty house."

"The main course is now about ready. You can line up for dinner as soon as you hear the band play 'The Bison Street Blues!' "

Everything was going well thanks to excellent back-up help and liaison from a very experienced and competent lady. But then, just as we were expecting the arrival on the grounds of the then Vice President Lyndon Johnson, this efficient helper was called to another part of the premises to see about the entertainment.

Some eager beaver butinski promptly rushed up to the place where I was presiding at the microphone and officiously informed me that the Vice President had arrived. As a result I gave the signal for the band to play "Eyes of Texas," for a group dressed as American Indians to move out to serve as a welcoming committee, and for the audience to be ready with their welcoming applause. An embarrassing wait ensued. I stalled and ad libbed but to no avail. The Vice President hadn't yet arrived and didn't in fact arrive until a half hour later. The inept volunteer had thrown a monkey wrench into what had up to then been a smoothly run affair. The lesson

I learned from that one was that at an event so large and important an M.C. needs a back-up man for his back-up man.

Some will say, "No harm was done."

But I believe in doing a thing of that kind right. I felt as annoyed as if I had agreed to play a serious piano solo for an important audience and, because of someone's carelessness, the piano bench collapsed in the middle of the number. *Newsweek* magazine, in writing up the party, accused me of being a bumbler, which I hardly appreciated.

Introduce Only a Few Men

An experienced federal judge recently asked my advice as to how to handle the introductions at a dinner at which he was to be Master of Ceremonies. He said that at a dinner of the same group the year before the M.C. had introduced so many fellow judges for a few remarks that a prominent Congressman who had been present when the speaking started became irked and left before he could be introduced.

"But what could the M.C. do?" my friend said. "All those federal judges at the dinner were very important."

"That's true," I told him. "But they aren't *elected!*" People who have to go out and run for their jobs feel they are entitled to special deference. In the case of Senators, members of Congress, and Governors, it is wise to give them priority attention.

It turned out about 150 men were expected at the dinner and my friend planned to introduce 40 or 50 of them individually. I pointed out that if he did it would not only bore everybody, but the 100 men who *weren't* introduced would be put out because they would consider they were equally as or more important than the 40 or 50 singled out.

I advised him not to introduce more than ten at most, assuming there was to be no speakers' table. If there was a speakers' table everyone sitting there should be introduced. But it is ridiculous to have a great long speakers' table for a small gathering.

A Trim Speakers' Table

One way to keep down the number at the speakers' table, where there are ladies present, is to have the wives (or husbands) of speakers' table guests sit together at special tables down in front. Then they don't have to be introduced.

If feasible the printed program should include a list of those at the speakers' table, preferably showing the position in which they are sitting. This is not easy to do since it requires that the programs be held up until a very short time before the event when all acceptances are firm. Even then one or two head table guests may be "no shows" at the last minute and the printed list then tells the audience that the group has been "stood up."

At a high-prestige affair, such as the Alfalfa Club annual dinner in Washington, "no shows" are unlikely, and each guest receives at his place a diagram of the entire banquet room showing the locations, not only of each one at the head table, but also of each of the 700 guests. This presents a tremendous chore in preparation but is a great boon to those present who, because of the nature of this top drawer affair, are interested in seeing who is there and in being located and seen themselves.

164

At such rare events as the Alfalfa Club and the Gridiron Club dinners, it is possible to list each name accurately, because each member is limited as to the number of guests he can invite and must furnish the names of each guest well in advance.

Where there may be some changes in the names of the guests, the brochure of those attending may be set up by table numbers and unknowns shown as "Guests of Mr. Frank Jones."

Guest List

It is absolutely essential, at significant political fund raising dinners, to provide each guest with a printed or mimeographed list showing each person attending, both alphabetically and by table number. Those who pay their $50 or $100 a plate to attend expect at least this much attention. They may want to be sure that some government or political figure to whom they are beholden has a way of determining readily that the particular person is there. Or they may want this tangible evidence of their support for future reference.

Even where the list of those at the speakers' table is printed and available to each guest, the master of ceremonies should always introduce each one at the head table orally. It is logical, and gracious, to do this immediately after the affair begins—right after the invocation at a luncheon or banquet. Then the audience can know whom they are looking at while they are eating.

Applause

But, no matter how pressed for time, the M.C. should *never, never* ask the audience to withhold their applause while he introduces the head table. How this insane practice ever got started I suppose we will never know. I think it began and flourished with nervous and inept M.C.'s who wanted to make people think they were highly experienced and efficient.

To begin with the practice is rude. The audience will probably applaud anyway for one or two guests. Then when the next fellow receives *no* applause or just a sickly ripple, it is embarrassing. The brittle type of M.C. then scolds the audience for not following his instructions and this creates tension.

Second, no time worth mentioning is really saved. Much more time can be saved by using care in choosing a minister who will keep the invocation short. Long invocations irritate and embarrass everybody. When President Johnson spoke before the American Bar Association in August, 1964, the preacher who gave the invocation went on so long I wasn't sure the President was going to be able to get "equal time."

The third and most important reason for letting people applaud those at the speakers' table, is that the purpose of having such a table is to provide recognition. And applause is a symbol of recognition.

Applause provides a feeling of importance and a sense of being appreciated. It makes no difference whether these reactions are completely rational and logical. The M.C. is dealing not with theory but with human nature.

Get the Name Right

It is for this reason that an M.C. cannot be too careful in pronouncing names correctly and giving titles accurately. No one is so busy he can't inquire in advance how an unusual name is pronounced and then put some do-it-yourself phonetic symbols beside the name on his notes.

One of the classic, completely true instances of botched up names happened some years ago when Ambassador Joseph Grew was presiding at a dinner to honor the retirement of Secretary of State George Marshall. General and Mrs. Eisenhower were among the noted guests at the head table. It was while Eisenhower was still on active duty in the army.

Grew was going all out in his praise of General Marshall.

"General Marshall has had a distinguished military and civilian record. He has been wartime Chief of Staff of the Army, Secretary of Defense, and Secretary of State. There is no honor within their command which the American people would not give him. But he refuses any further honors. All he wants to do is to go down to his beautiful farm in Virginia and spend the rest of his days with Mrs. Eisenhower."

After the explosion subsided and Grew had resumed his seat he passed down the table a little note to Mrs. Eisenhower which said:

"My apologies to the General."

She wrote on it: *"Which* General?"—and passed it back.

Everyone values his name. Never make puns about names. The bearer of the name has heard them all ad nauseam. The M.C. should take seriously the name of each head table guest he is introducing so that that person's brief few seconds in the limelight will not be marred with blundering and snickering and awkwardness.

The M.C. should also check personally right before he begins his introductions to be sure the head table is seated in the order shown on his list. To be introduced as someone else is a loss of face. It indicates that the person is not even known by the M.C.

A presiding officer must be firm.

He must not allow "too many bosses" to gum up the arrangements.

He must not allow "added starters" on the speaking program.

He must not accept last minute suggestions as to additional guests that should be introduced, additional telegrams that should be read, additional people that should be called on for a "few words."

A Good M.C. Is Vital

Good luncheon and dinner meetings do not just happen. A big part of their success is dependent on advance work and planning. But it is also vital to have an effective presiding officer. His jokes and his graciousness and his alertness are all keys to a good event. It is equally important that he be in control of the situation.

As soon as he begins to fumble and to be uncertain and apologetic, the hold on the audience weakens.

A prominent lady I know told me about an experience with an inept mistress of ceremonies in a Chicago suburb. First there was a pause of at least five minutes while the female M.C. whispered hoarsely to someone who came to consult with her at the podium. Then, finally getting around to presenting the prominent lady guest the M.C. said:

As you know Mrs. _____ has just recently moved back here from Washington where her husband held a very important government position. Mrs. _____ was very active and popular there and accomplished a great deal such as . . . let's see . . . oh, Mrs. _____ you please tell the audience just what it was you accomplished.

XXI

The Title of the Speech

The title of a speech can be important in drawing a crowd. When the crowd assembles they will not be particularly interested in the title as such. But the advance publicity and the printed program will, to a large extent, serve as the advance billing for the speech. If the title sounds interesting people will come.

For example, I have used as the title of this book *Humor in Public Speaking*. Why didn't I use *Suggestions on Improving Audience Interest in Public Speeches?*

Many years ago when I was on the staff of Adlai Stevenson while he was Governor of Illinois I learned a big lesson about writing and talking: eliminate unnecessary words. I learned that, after I had written something for use by Stevenson, it was important, before giving it to him, to go through it and cross out as many words as I could without changing the meaning. I might have written, for a county fair speech:

"I take the liberty of saying to you as I stand here today that in my opinion we may be facing a serious problem in the provision of adequate highway facilities for our rapidly expanding population."

All that could be boiled down to five words:

"We face a highway crisis."

Brevity Sells

A young fellow attempted to write an advertisement to describe a new kind of soap. Here's what he wrote: "The alkaline element and fats in this product are blended in such a way as to secure the highest quality of saponification, along with a specific gravity that keeps it on top of the water, relieving the bather of the trouble and annoyance of fishing around for it at the bottom of the tub during his ablutions. . . ." A more experienced writer later wrote the same thing in two words: *"It Floats!"*

The same thing applies to titles for speeches (and books and articles). If I had called this book "Suggestions on Improving Audience Interest in Public Speeches" the index cards in your local library would have catalogued this volume under "Suggestions" where it is very unlikely you or anyone else would have found it.

In addition, if by some accident you had run across

the title, you might well have said: how can I expect any real guide to pepping up speeches from someone who is so ponderous?

Short Words

Another thing that is important in speeches and titles is to avoid unnecessarily long words. If you have not had a chance to try it you will be floored by how much you can say by use of short words. The sentence you have just read, for example, is made up entirely of words of one syllable. I am convinced that a speech could be written using one syllable words only and that it would not sound at all childish or oversimplified.

Your title is the signboard for your speech. If the programs says Mr. Smith will speak on "Examples of asserted excessive restrictions in the economic area by government regulatory agencies," chances are many people will stay away because they will fear being subjected to a dull, academic lecture with a lot of overly complicated phraseology. However, if the title says simply "Overregulation of business," people are more likely to be interested. Unconsciously their reaction will be that anyone who can get to the point as simply and forcefully as that in the title will probably get down to brass tacks in discussing the problem.

Essentials

Here is a story to illustrate getting down to essentials.

An instructor in a college course on writing in England told the class that there were four essential subjects which should be brought into a successful work of fiction:

the deity, royalty, sex, and mystery. The instructor then gave the class three hours to compose an original short story. In five minutes a student in the front row handed in his paper and left the classroom. He had written:

"My God!" said the Duchess. "I'm pregnant. Who did it?"

Some titles sound so scholarly they serve to scare away ordinary listeners who will fear the talk will be overly academic and theoretical. Don't use: "An objective appraisal of the tenability of our military and economic position in Southeast Asia." Use instead "We should get out of Vietnam" or "We should go all out in Vietnam." It helps to tell the audience you are going to take a position, even though it may be one they disagree with.

While I was Postmaster General I was invited to the Bohemian Grove "encampment" north of San Francisco to make a Sunday afternoon "lakeside talk." This is a truly remarkable gathering. Top business, government, and cultural leaders from California and their guests from all over the country gather for two weeks each summer in a collection of camps in the redwood country in California. These tycoons themselves perform in plays, operettas, symphonies, and band concerts, which they have been writing and rehearsing for months in advance back in the exclusive, theater oriented Bohemian Club in San Francisco.

The "camps" are the furthest cry imaginable from "roughing it": permanent, spacious structures with the most modern plumbing, the most comfortable beds (with electric blankets), and the most completely stocked bars. The most exercise anyone gets is to walk to the sylvan theater for the theatrical events and to the large outdoor dining area under the trees where the wooden tables are covered with white table cloths and where a wine steward, key and all, is in attendance.

There is some strange fascination in California with intermingling outdoor rusticity and indoor luxury. At the ornate castle at San Simeon owned by William Randolph Hearst in his heyday, it was an ironclad rule that at even the most elegant formal dinners in the huge baronial hall, paper napkins were always used and catsup bottles were on the table. This was supposed to be in memory of the fact that in an earlier day, ante-castle and ante-Marian Davies, the Hearst family had used the site for country picnics.

But it is indeed an honor to be invited to talk at Bohemian Grove. Richard Nixon was on the program Saturday night and I was scheduled Sunday afternoon. I was to speak standing out in the open beside an attractive lake, with the audience lounging on the grass under the trees.

Weeks before the event my host asked me for the title of my talk. I hadn't had a chance to think about what I would say but, since he pressed me, I gave him a title which would cover anything I might decide on: "One hundred and twenty-nine days 'til Christmas."

It was a big mistake.

When I arrived at the camp—somewhat like entering a special millionaires' heaven—I found bulletin boards in strategic spots stating when I was going to speak and the title of my talk. I discovered I was going to be competing with numerous cocktail parties, bull sessions, and afternoon naps. I should have aroused curiosity with a

174

hard hitting title such as "Socialism can work," by which I would have been referring to the huge government-run, business-type operation which the Post Office is, or "Federal economy yes, penny pinching no." The latter was a title I used for a later speech after I left office which explained that while the Defense Department is given $150 million a day to spend, the traditional, nonglamorous domestic agencies, such as the Customs Bureau, are not allowed enough federal money to do their job. Customs doesn't even get enough to police narcotics smuggling.

The crowd at the lakeside talk was not as big as it might have been, and largely because I used a "blah" title which failed to arouse interest.

Title Draws

If the speech is to be delivered to a convention at a resort hotel, the delegates are not likely to get up to hear it if it is entitled "Developments in the Washington legislative picture affecting our industry during the current year," as they would be if the title were "The Dickerson Bill—threat to survival of our industry."

Speech titles should be like headlines—New York *Daily News* headlines. They should arouse interest. They should use hard hitting and positive words. They should express a point of view which will convince the potential listener he is going to hear some definite ideas and not just some inconclusive, wishy-washy generalities.

This doesn't mean the title has to give away what you are going to say, provided it arouses interest or curiosity.

An example of a title that arouses interest is one

that indicates you are going to predict the long-term future of the business or profession, or line of activity in which the audience is interested: "The Banking Business Fifty Years from Now"; "Where will the Railroads be in 30 years." This approach gives plenty of leeway for describing the problems and pitfalls in the particular field and at the same time weaving in some light material.

I had great success at a meeting of probate and trust lawyers at Champaign, Illinois, with a speech entitled "Estate Planning in the year 2000." There is even a humorous story on estate planning:

> A rich man had three married daughters but no grandchildren. One Sunday he invited the daughters and sons-in-law to dinner and after all were seated he asked them to bow their heads while he said grace.
>
> "Oh Lord," he said, "I give thanks for this fine family and I hope it may increase. To show my sincerity in being grateful for the blessing of family life I have asked my lawyer to draw up a trust to provide $200,000 for the parents of my first grandchild."
>
> After a few more sentences of reverent thanksgiving the man raised his head.
>
> The table was deserted.

XXII

The Art of Conversation

Why do I include this heading in a book on speechmaking?

The answer is basic to the reason why I have wanted to write this book. I want to urge people to talk, when making speeches, the same way they would talk to a group of friends at a luncheon for four.

They would not pontificate to these friends—or if they did they would have to find three other luncheon companions the next time.

An M.C., or a person making a speech, should follow the same rules which make for a good conversationalist.

Search your own experience and think of two or three people who are utterly boring to talk to. Why is it? What is it about their conversation that makes you want to slip away and talk to someone else?

Here are some of the common reasons:

1. Talking in a drab, colorless manner.
2. Complaining too much.
3. Having a chip on the shoulder.
4. Disliking too many people and too many things.
5. Talking too much about themselves.
6. Being too "know it all."
7. Using too many stilted expressions and affected phrases.
8. Being condescending—talking down to the listener.
9. Talking too long.
10. Talking on uninteresting subjects.
11. Being obscene.
12. Talking over the head of the listener.

Don't Be a Bore

The conversationalist every one wants to avoid is the fellow who gives endless, tiresome detail about his operation. In the course of doing it, he is not only drab and colorless but he complains too much, he talks too long, he talks too much about himself, and he talks on an oh so uninteresting subject.

The speaker who talks on his recent trip to Mexico can be just as boring if he concentrates on petty details of how his baggage got lost or how the fresh vegetables affected him.

The hallmark of the popular conversationalist is

one who is ingratiating, who is sensitive to the reactions of his listener and tries to key his remarks to what the listener wants to hear.

A person can improve his private conversation *by making an effort to have people like him*.

The same is true of speechmaking.

The speaker will do better if he tells himself: I want these people to like me. I'm not going to let them think I consider it a chore to talk to them. I'm not going to force something on them in which they are not interested. I'm not going to be "know it all" or condescending.

This doesn't mean, and I have stressed this elsewhere, that the speaker should kowtow to or butter up the audience. It is quite all right to tell them things they don't agree with provided you don't do it in an arrogant way.

Probably a person who is hopeless as a conversationalist will never be any better as a speaker. Both are manifestations of personality.

It is really discouraging to observe a sparkling, witty, and compelling conversationalist who—when he gets to a podium—shifts gears and becomes drab, tiresome, stilted, and stuffy. This indicates some emotional block or stage fright or ignorance of the secrets of speechmaking, any of which can be cured by the proper application of good advice.

Speeches Are General

A great deal of the more serious type of conversation and a large percentage of speeches are about public problems: high taxes, crime, juvenile delinquency, too much government, whether the moon race is worth the money, etc. But in speeches it is the usual thing only to describe the problem, to decry it, maybe to blame somebody, but almost never to give a concrete suggestion about something the members of the audience can do to alleviate the problem.

Part of this is because so many speechmaking programs are, for audience and speakers alike, merely mammoth exercises in stewing in their own juice. The speaker is saying things that those before him already agree with. They join in feeling displeasure and resentment about those who don't agree. But those who don't agree aren't present and will never hear, or hear of, the speech.

Even political speakers are orating most of the time during campaign swings to people who are already their followers. As a result of speaking to those who already agree, speakers are inclined to give cliché-ridden pep talks rather than reasoned arguments that can be used by their listeners.

For example, a speaker on law enforcement will spend 30 minutes bewailing the rising crime rate before an audience of solid citizens who seldom get so much as an overtime parking ticket. Such a speaker will end up saying that we must take a firm, united, courageous stand, and do *something*. He usually doesn't say *what*.

It would be better to end up with a suggestion that the group put on a testimonial dinner to honor the local police chief and show him the community is behind him in his efforts to fight crime.

Or a speaker, on "too much government" or "over-regulation," will spend most of his time explaining that we didn't have all these controls and laws and rules back in the days of George Washington and James Madison.

But he very seldom zeroes in on one or two specific cases (of which there are plenty) of excessive government interference. He may say "write your Congressman," but he seldom pinpoints even one law that the Congressman should try to have repealed.

Conversation Is Specific

Conversation is usually a quite different story. The "for instance," the horrible example, the personal experience are standard features of interesting conversation. A businessman doesn't sit around a luncheon table talking about the Founding Fathers and the Federalist Papers. He is more likely to say:

> Do you know that the National Labor Relations Board has held that a company can't close up and go out of business if it does it because its employees voted to join a union?

This is specific. It arouses interest. It makes the listeners start thinking.

Speeches would be better if they more closely resembled good conversation.

Here is a test. After you have your speech all prepared and someone asks you what you are going to cover in your speech, what will you say? Can you just "talk" it to them in such a way that they will be interested?

Will you merely say:

> I'm going to talk about education and point out that it has become too progressive and permissive.

Or will you say:

> I'm going to tell about a study that has been made showing that 40 per cent of the graduates from our local high

school last year were unable to pass a seventh grade spelling test given two weeks before they graduated. I'm going to outline a program that a group of citizens is proposing to the Board of Education to begin getting our public schools back to fundamentals. I'm going to explain what the new math did to a dozen of our high school juniors who worked as store clerks, trying to make change, last summer.

These headlines show that this speech is going to be like good conversation. It is going to bring the problem close to home, with specific, understandable examples, and it is going to suggest a solution.

The dull, pompous, stereotyped speaker, like the boring conversationalist, has difficulty seeing himself as others see him.

But if the "others" yawn, he should change his ways.

Being Specific

For a specific example of use of facts and statistics, woven into a talk without making it dull and pedantic, I include here a portion of a speech I have already mentioned in the chapter on "The Title of the Speech."

"ESTATE PLANNING IN THE YEAR 2000"
ESTATE PLANNING CONFERENCE
ILLINOIS STATE BAR ASSOCIATION
CHAMPAIGN, ILLINOIS

I have three reasons for choosing the title "Estate Planning in the Year 2000."

First, there are many of you up-to-the-minute specialists who know much more than I about Estate Planning in 1964. But I am just as much—and just as little—

an expert as anyone on Estate Planning in the year 2000.

Second, my title is meant to reflect a series of optimistic predictions. It says I don't expect in these next 36 years our civilization is going to be blown to bits by a superbomb. It says I do not expect our private enterprise economy to be replaced by Communism. It says also that I am not at all convinced that estate planning is going to be automated or done by electronic computers by the end of this century. My title says that I believe we are still going to need and have use for intelligent and careful estate planning *by lawyers* in private practice in that far off future year, 2000 A.D.

Third, my long-range projection into time gives me an excuse for discussing some of the big things I feel are going to affect the lawyer's problem in estate planning as the years go on.

Looking down the road to the far away year 2000, I think the estate planner is going to be faced with ever more challenging and prickly problems of tax impact. Whether we like it or not, the overall tax load, federal, state and local, is going to go up and up and up, regardless of which party is in office and regardless of how many electric lights are turned out.

I have two reasons for this dismal prediction.

The first has to do with the shift in the top needs of our society from those which can be provided by private financing to those which must necessarily be provided—if we are to have them at all—from public funds.

At the beginning of this century, the challenges ahead called for expanded farm output, new railroad lines, more steel capacity, expanded work force and the like—financed by private capital. Now the top needs we hear emphasized for the decades ahead are highways, schools, airports, rapid transit, water resources, housing for the poor and the elderly, war on poverty, more hospital beds, more recreational area, more capacity in colleges and universities, aid to underdeveloped countries, space exploration, and more sophisticated defense hardware— all of which must be financed in whole or to a predominant degree by *public* funds.

For example: In 1870, in the entire United States, only 8,000 students graduated from college. Last year there were over 50 times that many. Today there are about 3½ million students in college in this country. It is estimated that by 1985—in just 21 years—there will be 12 million students in college.

Just to provide the physical plant for this new surge of college entrants will cost nearly $90 billion!

A few of those billions will come from capital fund drives of private colleges. But most of the $90 billion must come from public funds.

Nearly everyone is for government economy *in general*—but for government *spending* in particular. Some who say Washington should economize by selling TVA turn right around without blinking an eye and demand that the federal government spend a billion dollars developing a supersonic commercial airplane. Some who deplore spending on farm programs have no hesitancy in supporting a bill such as is now pending in Congress for a brand new billion dollar Federal program for acquiring recreation areas. Some who say they oppose subsidies urge that the federal government pay for building local rapid transit systems.

We have just had a federal tax cut. But increases

in the Social Security payroll tax which would be required by the proposed Medicare program and other pending Social Security law changes, would more than cancel out the effect of the general tax cut for a self-employed person earning $7,000 a year.

The high point of inconsistency in talking about the government spending crisis is represented by those people, so numerous in Washington, who say they deplore federal budget deficits but who insist that the defense budget and the space budget are sacrosanct or should be even bigger.

The incredible pressures on Washington officials to keep defense and space spending high for economic and employment reasons are dramatically described in a new novel, *Convention,* by the authors of *Seven Days in May.* I recommend this book in a gesture of bipartisanship. It is about a Republican national convention in some unspecified future year.

Between now and the year 2000 that I am talking about, approximately 19 million minutes will tick by on the clock. That seems like an enormous figure—and it is. But it is the number of dollars which are spent by the Defense Department alone every three hours of every day! I suggest you keep that in mind if you are really interested in understanding the government spending situation. It puts a different light on some of the stories we read—about how *one* million dollars was saved by some ballyhooed nondefense economy move or other such as closing down the San Francisco Mint several years ago so that we now have a nationwide coin shortage.

The conventional, basic, nonglamorous, nondefense functions of the federal government are being squeezed to death budgetwise because so much of the money goes for defense and space and other more dramatic programs. Just as one example, year after year the Congress denies to the Customs Bureau the money it needs to prevent smuggling of narcotics.

A little noticed aspect of the overall tax problem is the skyrocketing of state and local government spending, employment and debt. State and local government spending has gone up over 500 per cent since World War II. In the same period employment by state and local governments has gone up 3½ million, and debt of these units of government has gone up 450 per cent. In Pennsylvania school districts already levy personal income taxes. I fully expect that by the year 2000 Mosquito Abatement Districts will be levying inheritance taxes.

Spending and taxes at all levels of government are bound to keep rising. Tax loopholes will be harder to come by. The estate planner of the decades ahead will to an increased degree have to be preoccupied with tax impact.

Yet I believe in the coming 36 years the rich will continue to get richer, our average standard of living will continue to rise to an astounding extent, we really will get rid of most of our poverty, and both the public and the office holders will continue to *talk* government economy and to *practice* government spending.

And some of us, who may still be around in the year 2000, will look back to 1964 as "the good old days" when life was sweet and simple, when tax laws were relatively uncomplicated, when the law schools still devoted more time to the Rule in Shelley's case than to use of settlement options in life insurance contracts, when the dollar was still worth 47 cents, when the Dow-Jones average was a mere 820, and when the Federal budget was at the incredibly low figure of $98 billion. And as scholars of the first year of the twenty-first century ponder the doubling of population since 1964 to 350 million people in the United States, 20 million in Illinois, and over 7 billion in the world they may conclude that the most significant force in the last third of the 20th century was *not* atomic energy but a much more basic and earlier discovered type of energy.

The indications are that the coming 36 years of population explosion will smile much more kindly on planned estates than they will on planned parenthood.

XXIII

$\mathcal{H}$umor $\mathcal{T}$ied to $\mathcal{O}$ccupations

There are many stories on the theme of entering heaven. This one for example can be used for nearly any gathering of a professional or specialized business group. For example it might be used at a bankers' convention.

Bishops

A bishop died and went to heaven. As he approached the pearly gates he saw a long line waiting. He stood in line several hours and then sent an angel up to the gate to tell St. Peter that an important bishop had arrived. Still nothing happened.

Finally the angel came back and said there would be more delay because there was a big special celebration to welcome Joseph T. Potts, the president of a bank. The bishop bridled and demanded:

"What's so special about him? I've served the church for 40 years. Why should I have to be delayed by him?"

"Well, you see," said the angel, "we get bishops up here every few weeks but this is the first bank president we've ever had."

In another version the arrival getting all the attention is a New York (or Detroit, or San Francisco) taxi driver. He gets special attention and when the bishop complains he is told:

"He's scared Hell out of more people *every day* with his driving than you've done in any *month* with your sermons."

Accountants

Brown rose through the ranks to become the head of a great accounting firm. Their business grew phenomenally and their clients and offices multiplied.

Only one thing about Brown mystified his colleagues. From his earliest days and continuing right up through his sensational success, he had a strange habit. He arrived at his office early every morning and without saying a word to anybody went to his desk, took a little key from his pocket, unlocked and opened the center drawer, unfolded and looked briefly at a piece of paper inside, and then carefully refolded the paper and closed and locked the drawer again. Then the day's work began.

This went on for years. No one could figure out what was in the desk, or could get a peek inside it. Then Brown died. After a delay barely short enough to show due respect, the colleagues converged on the desk. Some work with a paper knife took care of the lock. Expectantly they opened the drawer. Inside was just one little piece of paper. They hurriedly unfolded it and spread it on the desk. On it was written, in Brown's handwriting:

"The debit side is the one nearest the window."

Doctors

Jones had a serious liver ailment which demanded expert surgery. He inquired as to the best man for the job and was told that a doctor who lectured at Johns Hopkins Medical School was the one outstanding specialist on this particular operation. Jones went to Johns Hopkins and had the job done. Shortly after he came out of the anesthetic the surgeon came in to check up.

"How's your side feel?" he asked cheerily.

"Oh my side's all right," Jones said. "But I have a terrible pain in my throat."

"Never mind that," said the doctor. "Let me take a look at those dressings."

"But doctor," Jones croaked. "My throat. What's wrong with it?"

"Well," sighed the doctor. "I guess I'll have to tell you. Now just relax and you'll understand. You know how I told you I do my operations in that big amphitheater with all the medical students looking on. It's a tense situation with all those eyes looking over your shoulder and every cut and every stitch being watched. Now yours was a most unusual case—and very serious.

I've only had one other patient with this very same thing in all my practice, and most doctors never see it in a lifetime. It was a long procedure—nearly two hours. But luck was with me, and my hand was steady. I had a perfect result. When it was over and I stood back from the table, the amphitheater burst into applause. The medical students stood on their feet and cheered. In fact, the acclaim was so deafening and went on so long that—well —I took out your tonsils for an encore."

Entertainers

Back in the days when the late Ezio Pinza was known far and wide for his starring role in "South Pacific," a man who resembled him somewhat got out of a cab in front of a large hotel.

The doorman rushed up obsequiously.

"Welcome, Mr. Pinza. Let me take your suitcase. We're expecting you!"

Taken aback, the man said:

"No. No. I'm not Pinza. My name is Sam Ginzberg!"

When the man entered the lobby the room clerk nearly fell over the counter in the effusiveness of his greeting.

"Welcome, Mr. Pinza. It's a great honor to have you here. You are already registered in. The bellboy here will take you right up to your suite."

"No. No. Sam Ginzberg. Not Pinza. I'm Sam Ginzberg."

With many flourishes the bellboy showed him to the elevator and here again there was the fawning greeting to Pinza and Ginzberg's frustrated denial.

When they arrived at the top floor the bellboy opened the door of the best suite. Inside was a glamorous blonde stretched on a chaise longue.

"Mr. Pinza!" she bubbled. "I've been waiting for you!"

"No. No. Sam . . . Sam . . . *Sam Enchanted Evening!*"

Executives

Mr. Chairman and Fellow Salesmen:*

From that introduction, you know that I am a Vice President—but I don't use my title except when I send letters that are official. There's a good reason for this. It came about as the result of a visit with a sales group in Eastern Pennsylvania. At the conclusion of the meeting, we had an old fashioned picnic-type supper. Except in the Middle West, I've never seen as much food as the wives brought in. After the meal, the chairman had a few words to say and introduced me. I noticed that, as I spoke, a lady right close to me listened intently to every word and watched every gesture. When the meeting was over, she came up to me and said she'd like to ask me a question. I said, "Well, go ahead." She said, "I'd like to ask you *how* you got your job." Sort of rocked me back on my heels and I said, "What do you mean, how did I get my job?" She said, "Well, it's this way: I have a son who is 16 and I've been doing a lot of thinking about what he might do in life. He isn't good looking enough to get into television, he's too lazy to do manual

---

*From remarks of James E. Rutherford, Vice President in charge of Mid-America Operations, Prudential Insurance Company of America, at luncheon of Illinois State Bar Association, November 30, 1956.

labor and he isn't smart enough to be a salesman like his father. You know, as I've watched you here this evening, I've concluded that *you* have the very job for which he's fitted."

Insurance

A lady didn't quite make it in her rush to the hospital and her baby was born on the hospital front lawn.

Weeks later when the hospital bill came it included an item: "Delivery Room, $25.00." The lady fired the bill right back with an angry explanation of what had happened.

Promptly she received a revised bill with an item: Green's Fee, $25.00."

———•—•—•———

Ginsberg and Epstein met each other while sitting in the sun at a Florida resort. They began telling their respective life histories.

Ginsberg was first:

I had the very finest department store in all southern New Jersey. Carried only the best merchandise. Very successful. And then the chains came in. Cheap merchandise, cut-rate prices. It was a struggle. And then when it seemed things couldn't get any worse the store burned to the ground. It was a tragedy. But I collected the insurance and got ready to rebuild. Then my wife and my children came to me and they said "Papa. You have already worked too hard. You have struggled. You have fought the chains. You have worried and worn yourself out. Why don't you just retire and we'll all move to Florida?" So I did, and here I am.

Epstein: Very, very interesting, and such a coincidence. My story is much the same. I had a fine factory in Ohio. Top quality products. Very successful. And then the unions came. Big demands. Costs shooting up. It was a struggle. And then we had a flood and my factory was totally destroyed. I collected the insurance and got ready to rebuild. But my wife and children came the same way, pointed out how I had worried and struggled and suggested I retire. I did and here I am.

Ginsberg: Very interesting. (*Then a long pause*) Do you mind if I ask you something?

Epstein: No, go right ahead.

Ginsberg: Just how do you start a flood?

Lawyers

Two law partners had a very tough court case which involved a large amount of money. One of the partners had to leave town on a business trip and he asked his partner to wire him as soon as the case was decided. After he had been away a few days he received this telegram:

"Justice has prevailed."

He immediately wired back:

"Appeal at once."

Stockbrokers

Winterbottom's stockbroker telephoned and told him of a new stock that was coming out: Dynamic Seed Company. It was available at only $3 a share. Winterbottom bought 200 shares.

A few days later the broker called and said the stock was quoted at $4.50 and that "it was going up." Winterbottom bought 200 more shares.

Next day the quote was $6 and the next day $8.

The broker kept calling. It was going up, he said: $10, $12, 15. Each time the broker called Winterbottom bought 200 more shares.

Finally when the broker called and announced excitedly it was at $16 Winterbottom said decisively "Sell it all."

"Sell?" said the broker incredulously. "To *whom!*"

Teachers

Ryan was a good high school English teacher but he had a bad habit of frequenting bars. One night about 1 A.M. in a local saloon he began regaling two men standing next to him.

"I've been listening to you birds talk," he said. "And you murder our wonderful English vocabulary. You say *aggravated* when you mean *irritated* and you say *frustrated* when you mean *aggravated!*"

"So what?" the fellow drinkers replied. "They all mean the same thing."

"Oh no they don't any such thing. Now just let me give you a simple demonstration of the difference. See that telephone there on the end of the bar. All right. Now I'm going to just pick out a number at random and dial it. AB. 2-3456. Now you two listen over my shoulder. Hello. Hello. Is Wigglesworth there?

A sleepy voice answered: "No, no, you have the wrong number. Be more careful what you're doing. You woke me up out of a sound sleep."

Ryan put down the phone.

"Now that fellow was *irritated*," he said.

In about 15 minutes he carefully dialed the same number again.

"Hello, is Wigglesworth there?"

"Oh, blast you, you have the wrong number. Get away from that phone and go to bed. This is the second time I've been awakened from a sound sleep."

"Now he is *aggravated*," said Ryan as he hung up.

He carefully waited another 15 minutes before dialing the same number a third time. When the sleepy voice answered, he said in a polite tone:

"Hello, this is Wigglesworth. Do you have any messages for me?"

There was silence at the other end as Ryan hung up.

"*Now* that fellow is *frustrated*," he said.

XXIV

Churches and Clergy

A successful businessman became more and more harassed, took to drink, and went to pot. Finally he was put in a sanitarium. He found that very tiresome and in a few weeks told the manager of the place that he was cured.

"What are you going to do when you get out?" asked the manager.

The man's eyes sparkled.

"I'm going to work hard and make a lot of money and then I'm going to throw a cocktail party with a bar 40 feet long and I'm going to catch up!"

"You're not cured," said the manager impatiently. "You stay right here."

In a few weeks the businessman again claimed that he was cured. The manager asked him the same question.

"I'm going to work hard and make a lot of money and build a fine house for my family."

"That sounds good. What then."

"In that house I'm going to have a great big wine cellar. I'm going to fill it with the best liquor there is. And I'm going to catch up!"

"Back to your room," said the manager. "And don't pester me any more."

The businessman waited a month and then approached the manager again and told him he was cured.

"Now what are you going to do when you get out?" said the manager irritably.

"I'm going to work hard and make a lot of money. I'm going to use it to educate my children. I'm going to use my spare time to be active in my church and the Red Cross and the Y.M.C.A."

"That sounds pretty good. Now for a few follow-up questions. What does White Horse mean to you?"

"White Horse? Why White Horse was the horse Sir Galahad rode. He was one of the most idealistic men that ever lived."

"OK. How about Gordon's?"

"Gordon's? Gordon's? Gordon was a great British general in the first World War. He was a fine, clean living gentleman."

"Good. How about Fleishmanns?"

"Fleishmann is a yeast. It's very healthful, very good for you."

"Well, you're doing all right. Now for one final question. How about Vat 69?"

"Vat 69? Vat 69? Oh yes, Vat 69 is the Pope's telephone number."

———•••———

A very nationalistic Irish priest was assigned to a parish in the heart of London. Each Sunday in his sermon, he attacked the English as being betrayers, traitors, and underhanded schemers. There were many complaints and the bishop repeatedly warned him to stop. But he kept right on: the English were betrayers, etc.

Finally the bishop told him:

"One more sermon like that and you will be defrocked."

The following Sunday the priest began his sermon as follows:

"My sermon today will be on the Last Supper."

There was a murmur of appreciation from the congregation.

"The Master was sitting at the table with his apostles. He said to them: 'One of you is betraying me.'

"Peter looked up in anguish and said: 'You don't think it is me do you, Master?'

" 'No, I know it is not you.'

"James said: 'You don't think I'm the one, do you, Master?'

" 'No, James, I know it is not you. The same with Thomas.'

"Then Judas spoke up: 'Hi say there Guvnur, you don't think Hi'm the blighter, do you?' "

———•••———

A Jewish father who had not been a great success pinned all his hopes on his son. He hoped the boy would excel in school and go on to great things.

199

But the boy wasn't interested in studying. He scraped along and then in eighth grade flunked out of public school entirely. The father was desperate. He didn't have enough money to send the boy to private school and yet the boy had to have an education if he was to be the great success the father hoped. As a last resort the father went to see a neighboring priest and persuaded him to give the boy a chance at the Catholic school.

After a few months the boy brought home his report card. With trembling fingers the father opened it. The grade for every Subject was an "A."

"Abie, what happened?" the father asked in amazement.

"Well, papa, when I went over to that priest's office, the first thing I saw was that sort of statue hanging there on the wall over his desk—that poor Jewish boy with blood on him. And I said to myself: 'These people *mean business!*'"

———•◆•———

A youthful admiral and an Episcopal bishop were each pacing nervously outside the maternity section of a hospital.

Finally a nurse came out and said to the admiral:

"You have just become the father of a fine eight-pound boy. He is perfect in every respect. And he looks just like you: a long body, a high forehead, brown hair.

The admiral beamed and throwing back his shoulders said:

"I'm going back to the ship and fire a 15-gun salute."

He left and the bishop continued to pace nervously.

After a bit the nurse came out again:

"Bishop, you too are the father of a fine boy. He is

perfect in every respect. Of course, he doesn't look much like you. He has reddish hair and a round head and a short body."

The bishop looked at her grimly and said:

"I'm going back to the rectory and fire a canon."

———•—•—•———

Two bright English boys became bitter rivals and enemies during their days at "public school." Their intense dislike for each other continued down through the years. One became a noted admiral and the other became an Anglican bishop. The bishop became quite rotund.

One day the bishop, dressed in a long clerical robe, spotted the admiral, decked out in his uniform, on a railroad station platform.

"Conductor," he said to the admiral, in a disdainful voice. "Could you tell me when the next train leaves for Leicester?"

The admiral spotted his enemy but did not let on.

"Certainly madame," he replied. "It leaves in an hour. But in your delicate condition I wonder if you should be traveling."

———•—•—•———

A sanctimonious priest noticed that one of his prominent parishioners seldom came to confession, and he spoke to him about it.

"I live a very quiet life, father," said the man. "I don't have much chance to meet temptation. I try to do what's right."

"But," the priest pressed him, "haven't you ever done anything really bad—something you're deeply ashamed of?"

The man scratched his head.

"I can't think of anything."

"Oh, there must be something—in your early life perhaps?"

The man thought some more.

"Well, when I was a boy I did take an air rifle and shot a little bird."

The following Sunday the priest was giving his sermon.

"Even in our own parish we have examples of virtue that should inspire us. Take for example our distinguished Mr. Flaherty. He leads an exemplary life. He still has on his sensitive conscience the one misdeed of which he has been guilty. Many, many years ago he shot a little bird."

Flaherty jumped to his feet, his face flushed.

"OK blabber-mouth," he shouted. "Now you know why I didn't really tell you anything."

A distressed Jewish father went to see his rabbi and told him this tale of woe:

"I have a fine son, a very intelligent, kind-hearted boy. I have raised him carefully in the ways of our Jewish faith. I have taught him the traditions and ways of our great people. We have carefully observed all the holidays. Then he grew up and finished school and went out into the world. And suddenly he decided to become a Christian. He has turned his back on our faith."

The rabbi sighed wanly and said:

"It's a funny thing you would come to me. Exactly the same thing has happened to me. I too have a fine boy. He was the apple of my eye. I brought him up in all the Jewish traditions. He too finished school and went out into the world. And then he too decided to become a Christian and leave our faith."

"Then what did you do," said the distressed father.

"I went to the temple and I prayed to our God. I told Him the whole story just as I have told it to you."

"And what happened?"

"After I had finished praying and telling my story, I'm sure I heard a voice from high up in the temple say: 'It's a funny thing you would come to me.' "

———•◄•►•———

A Texan was riding on a train heading up North. A Jewish man was seated facing him. As the day wore on, the Texan reached up to the baggage rack and took down a large paper sack. He removed a bulging ham sandwich, took a bite from it, and then noticing the Jewish man eyeing him, took another ham sandwich from the sack and offered it.

"Is it Kosher?" said the Jewish gentleman.

"What do you mean 'is it Kosher,' " said the Texan irritably.

"If it isn't Kosher, I won't eat it."

"Listen. I grew the hogs for this ham right on my own ranch down in Texas. They were born on my ranch. I gave them all the best of care, the best food, the best water. I slaughtered them myself right in my own slaughter house, butchered them myself, hung the hams in my own smoke house. This bread in these sandwiches, my wife made it right in our own kitchen. I grew the wheat myself and ground it. What do you mean Kosher."

"If it is not Kosher I won't eat it," said the Jew with finality.

With a surly look, the Texan reached down again

into the sack and pulled out a bottle and two paper cups. He poured some purple liquid into one of the cups and offered it to his companion.

"Have some wine," he barked.

"Is it Kosher?" the Jew asked stubbornly.

"Is it Kosher! Is it Kosher! Now listen to this. I grew these grapes on my own vines. I crushed them on my own ranch, all by the most sanitary methods. I sterilized the bottles before I used them. This is the very best. What do you mean Kosher?"

"If it's not Kosher, I won't drink it."

The Texan pulled out a big six-shooter, pointed it at the Jewish gentleman and said menacingly:

"Drink that wine!"

The Jewish gentleman took the paper cup and as he began to drink the wine said:

"While you've got me covered would you mind passing me that ham sandwich?"

———•◆•◆•———

XXV

Human Nature

Three internationally famous nuclear scientists, a German, an Englishman, and a Jew had been working together at a research base. Without warning they each began to experience fever and fatigue and were examined by the base medical officer.

After a painstaking examination, he addressed them with a long face.

"You have all obviously become accidentally exposed to serious radioactivity. You each have no more than a month to live. With those few priceless weeks, you should be thinking what you want to do. The base will pay all your expenses."

The German scientist was first to reply.

"I want to go back to my ancestral home in Bavaria and sit in the garden of my old university and drink beer with my comrades and think of my heritage from my distinguished ancestors."

The Englishman was next.

"I want to go to Dover, charter a boat, and sail out onto the North Sea so that I can view the White Cliffs and think of the glorious heritage of my native land."

The Jewish scientist was last.

"I want to go back to the Bronx—and see another doctor!"

———•◦•———

A Baptist minister applied for membership in the local Rotary Club.

"We only take one member from each line of work," they told him politely. "We already have a preacher. In fact the only opening we have is for a hog caller."

"OK, I'll take that," was the reply. "I'm usually known as the shepherd of my flock. But you know your membership better than I do."

———•◦•———

A man paced nervously outside the maternity ward of a Catholic hospital. A solicitous nun approached to offer him reassurance.

"Will this be your first child?" she asked kindly.

"Oh, no, ma'am. We already have nine children."

"Wonderful! What a fine, devout family. What parish do you belong to?"

"No parish, ma'am. I'm a Methodist."

The sister walked away rapidly, visibly upset, and said to another nun in the corridor:

"Be careful of that man walking up and down in the reception room. I think he's a sex maniac!"

———— • • • ————

The Lone Ranger and Tonto were riding along in unfamiliar country. Suddenly far up ahead they saw a large band of unfriendly Indians.

"What do we do now," said the Lone Ranger.

"Ride south," said Tonto.

So they turned hurriedly and galloped south. But in a few miles, they again saw in the distance a band of unfriendly Indians.

"What do we do now?" said the Lone Ranger.

"Ride east," said Tonto.

But after they rode east a few miles the same thing happened.

"What do we do now?"

"Ride west."

Again they galloped off. But this time at a much closer range they saw the largest band of all of unfriendly Indians.

"What do we do now?" shouted the Lone Ranger in great excitement.

Tonto was calm.

"What do you mean *we?*"

———— • • • ————

Using the above story as an example, we can see how a particular joke theme can be adapted to many different situations.

In early 1961, immediately after taking office, President Kennedy was informed that the Democratic Party campaign deficit was nearly $4,000,000. Kennedy said to Matt McCloskey, Democratic Party Treasurer: "What do you suppose we would have done about this if we had lost?"

Mr. McCloskey replied: "Where do you get that 'we' stuff? *I'd* probably have gone to Norway." (New York *Herald Tribune,* January 22, 1961.)

Many wisecracks and quick retorts are adaptations of stories involving a parallel situation. This is particularly true of comebacks to trite, stereotyped statements:

"Money won't buy friends."

"No, but it gives you a better class of enemies."

———•—•—•———

"Papa," said Abie, Jr., reading a school book. "What does the word 'ethics' mean?"

"Well, I'll give you an example," says Abie. "Let's say I'm waiting on a customer in the store. He buys something, hands me a ten dollar bill, and I give him change. Just as he is walking out the door and I'm putting the money in the cash register, I notice there are two ten dollar bills stuck together.

"Now, that's a question of ethics. Should I tell my partner?"

———•—•—•———

A man had a dog that was so intelligent that each guest who observed it insisted he should send the animal away to school. At first he pooh-poohed the suggestion but his friends were so unanimous that finally he arranged to do as they said.

After a year the dog arrived home and walked in the front door.

"Did you do well in school?" said the man.

The dog nodded his head.

"What did you study, history?"

The dog shook his head disdainfully.

"Mathematics?"

Again the dog shook his head.

"Foreign language?"

This time the dog nodded his head in an enthusiastic affirmative.

"Say something in a foreign language."

"Meow!" said the dog proudly.

———•◆•———

A rich farmer at a county fair sideshow saw an act starring a talking dog and a talking chicken. When it was over he rushed backstage and said to the act's owner:

"I'll give you a thousand dollars for that chicken. It will be worth it to surprise my neighbors."

"That's very generous," said the carnival man, "but I couldn't part with that chicken."

"I'll make it two thousand."

"No. I can see you're an honest man. I wouldn't want to play you for a sucker. I always tell the truth. That chicken can't really talk."

"But I *heard* it talk with my very own ears."

"No. It can't talk. You see it just seemed that way. The fact is the dog is a ventriloquist."

———•◆•———

Thompson was walking across a bridge when he noticed a dozing fisherman.

"There's a bite on your line," Thompson said, nudging the fisherman.

"Sure enough," said the man. "Thanks. Say, would you mind reeling the line in for me?"

Thompson obliged, landed a nice fish, and turned to go.

"Oh, say," said the man. "Would you mind taking him off the hook?"

Again Thompson obliged.

"I suppose you want me to bait the hook again, is that right?"

"Oh, yes. You're so kind," said the fisherman drowsily.

"You're the laziest man I ever saw," said Thompson. "What you need is to get married and have a little boy who can wait on you and pull in your fish."

"Yes, you're right," said the fisherman, "do you know where I could find a pregnant woman?"

———•••———

XXVI

Publicity

Publicity for a speechmaking event is a big subject in itself but here are a few pointers and pitfalls:

What are the purposes and goals of the publicity?

1. To advertise and build prestige for the sponsoring organization.
2. To recognize and honor the speaker, particularly if he is appearing for no fee.

The important thing to realize is what publicity will *not* do. Except in the most unusual cases it will not produce a crowd or an audience. If mis-

cellaneous members of the public read in the paper that
W. W. Wigglesworth, head of the sociology department
at the state university, is going to speak at the Community
Chest kick-off luncheon on "Juvenile Delinquency," these
members of the public are not going to come uninvited to
hear the speech. However, careful efforts should be made
to obtain maximum publicity for the event. It helps to call
attention to the Community Chest drive. And it is a form
of "payment" to Professor Wigglesworth for coming to
make the speech.

If the speaker is to be Bobby Kennedy or Richard
Burton or John Glenn, rank and file members of the public will come of their own volition because of the glamour
of the name. But such drawing cards are few and far
between and not likely to be the speakers at the type of
event I am talking about.

One time when I was trapped into making a speech
in too large an auditorium, and the audience was, as I
predicted, disappointingly small, the officious program
chairwoman tried to excuse the situation by saying it was
due to a protracted newspaper strike in that particular
city. Assuming she was sincere in using that alibi, it
shows that she completely misconceived what newspaper
publicity would have achieved for her. It was a fund raising event with an admission charge of $5 a head. It is
inconceivable that any more than a handful of people,
even if the newspapers had been publishing, would have
appeared and paid $5 just because they read about the
event.

Go Get the Crowd

It is up to the organization and those in charge of
the event to produce the crowd, normally from having a

regular clientele of members or supporters. If this isn't enough there should be a telephone campaign to stir up interest. Bulletins or form letters will not do the trick unless they are followed up.

At a Federal Bar Association Convention in Washington the final day fell on a Saturday and those in charge became worried about the small demand for tickets for that last day's luncheon. Federal Judge Sarah Hughes, the lady who swore in Lyndon Johnson as President, was to be honored at that luncheon and it was important to have a respectable turnout. Instead of sitting around ringing her hands, the livewire lady running the event asked a number of people such as myself to come to the luncheon and obtained definite commitments. No amount of publicity would have caused one to go. I went and so did plenty of others. It was an overflow crowd and well worthwhile.

The program chairman, as soon as he obtains an acceptance from the principal speaker, should request glossy print photographs and a biographical sketch. If the speaker is written up adequately in *Who's Who in America* or in one of the regional *Who's Who* volumes, it may flatter the speaker to ask him if it is agreeable with him for that biography to be used. The local newspapers may already have photographs of the speaker in their files, but it is a good idea to allow the speaker to submit a picture which is his current preference.

If the event is special, such as the annual dinner of the Red Cross, or a visit by the current president of Rotary International, the person in charge of publicity should not trust to a routine mailing to the newspapers of the picture and biography. He should take them over and put them into the hands of the managing editor or the highest ranking member of the editorial staff he can get in to see. If the speaker is a prominent business leader, the handouts should be delivered to the financial editors of each of the newspapers.

Personal Approach

There should be a little sales pitch delivered in person to tell why the event is newsworthy. Tell the newsman why it is a good story which will be worth *his* while, not why the organization wants some free publicity which will will be worth *its* while.

Business newspaper offices and particularly financial editors are deluged with mass produced, self-serving press releases which pile up on desks and most of which are never used.

The biography of the speaker should, if too long and dreary, be pruned and brightened up before it is turned over to the press. It should stress public service aspects of the man's life, not merely that he is a highly effective money maker or technician. You can notice from the obituary pages how newspapers stress the public service side of people's lives. Even if the man has been making a huge income as a corporation lawyer for many years, the press write-up is more likely to headline his wartime service as regional head of the O.P.A. or his role as a member of the U.S. Olympic Committee.

The material given to the press should include, not just the speaker's picture and biography, but other details about the program and the organization which will make the story readable, such as names of prominent guests who will be present. The purpose is to make the program sound interesting so that the regular membership and supporters will come and will urge others to come and will bring guests.

Don't stop just with newspaper publicity. In nearly every city there are one or more radio or TV stations which carry live interviews with significant people when they come to town. The interview can be taped at a time convenient for the speaker, or if he is pressed for time a radio station can often use a few sentences on a telephone interview as part of a news broadcast. Some stations carry a daily feature of announcements of coming events in the community.

The organization itself probably has a newsletter or regular bulletin to members and contributors. The coming program should be written up in this publication in a way that will arouse interest.

Don't write it like this:

> The speaker at the annual dinner will be W. W. Wigglesworth. Professor Wigglesworth holds an A.B. degree from Williams, an M.A. degree from the University of Arizona and a Ph.D. degree from the University of Missouri. He is a member of the American Sociological Society and is the author of a book on juvenile delinquency.

Try for something like this:

> Dr. W. W. Wigglesworth, whom we have succeeded in getting as our speaker for the annual dinner, is known as the "bombshell of sociology." His articles insisting that juvenile delinquents are being mollycoddled by our courts have caused intense debate in law enforcement and university circles. He recently returned from a White House Conference on "Crime in the Streets," where he urged a get-tough policy against young lawbreakers. The Civil Liberties Union has

demanded the ouster of Dr. Wigglesworth from his post as head of the Sociology Department at the State University.

Speaker's Biography

Not every Community Chest speaker will have an exciting biography. But in writing him up make it as interesting as possible by describing, if there is such, some lively controversy in which the speaker has been engaged. Or make him sound colorful or amusing. Don't just recite cold statistics about him, particularly a long list of academic qualifications.

If the speaker at an event of local importance has a book in print try to interest local book stores in featuring the book in displays and newspaper advertisements with a reference to the approaching speaking engagement.

Don't take the publicity for granted. Try to have it handled by an experienced hand or at least by someone who will seek expert advice.

For some reason many people with no public relations know-how consider themselves to have become infallible public relations experts by a process of osmosis. When the speaking event arrives and not a word about it has appeared in print such a person may say:

> I sent a copy of the speaker's biography to the publisher of the newspaper marked "personal and confidential." I don't understand why the paper didn't print a word of it.

It just happens the publisher has been in Europe for the previous four weeks. There was never a follow-up telephone call by the publicity chairman or a visit to the newspaper office.

XXVII

Substitutes for Speeches

Various substitutes for speeches are tried either because desirable speakers can't be lined up or because there is an effort to achieve change of pace.

As a result nearly every convention of more than one day duration has one or more "panels." And many have debates; closed circuit TV presentations; speeches made by an out of town speaker by telephone; question periods; "press conferences," which the delegates to the convention can attend; moving pictures, film slides, and sometimes skits; and "stump the experts" question and answer contests, or other adaptations of TV techniques.

Panels are usually not in fact a substitute for speeches. Because most panelists, no matter how they are exhorted, insist on making full-fledged prepared speeches, one after another, so that all the time is used up before there can be any discussion.

Part of the trouble is that there are usually at least four and sometimes more members of the panel. Then there is a "moderator," who also is usually carried away by the presence of a microphone and not only makes a speech himself but also makes a long introduction of each panel member.

The only way you can make a panel work is by having the members' presentations five minutes long at most, and then having some lively discussion among them and with questioners in the audience.

How can a moderator make a panel member stop talking after five minutes without hurting his feelings?

Use Humor

Have the moderator set up some silly gimmick which will remind the panelist in some obvious and good-natured way that his time is up. For example, there can be a big alarm clock near the podium which will go off loudly after five minutes. Or a large hour glass. Or, on signal from the moderator, all the other panelists can stand up and remain standing at the end of five minutes.

More elaborately, the public address system can be rigged so that the amplification stops when five minutes are up. In addition an unlikely and laugh-provoking voice may suddenly take the place of the speaker's after five minutes, such as a recording of a Khrushchev speech or a Beatles' rendition.

If the moderator establishes the right atmosphere for this sort of interruption, it will be accepted in a good-natured way and will not insult the panelists. After all, United States Senators and Congressmen have set up rules under which they are reminded publicly, sometimes in mid-sentence, that "time is up."

It will accomplish nothing to get the panelists' set speeches stopped if it is then impossible to get discussion started.

The best way to provoke discussion is to have a lively topic about which people on opposite sides will have strong feelings. At a convention of life insurance agents (not a convention put on by their employer) a discussion of expansion of group insurance can start some fireworks if a home office man who favors group can be pitted against a top salesman who finds it is cannibalizing his business.

Whom to Invite

For this reason it is well to avoid panel members, such as high government officials, who are too important or too dignified to join in a no-holds-barred give and take. Sometimes two Congressmen, who are on opposite sides of an issue, will agree to debate the subject before a trade association or similar audience. A warning here, however: members of Congress are notorious last minute "no shows" for speaking engagements. Congress now meets on practically a year-round basis and there are unpredictable debates and votes on key bills which keep the members from meeting the out of town engagements.

In addition to a lively topic, and panelists who are fair game for hard hitting disagreement, a valuable assist may be given to panel discussions and audience question and answer periods by planted questions.

Have a few good questions ready that can be used to stir up discussion until the give and take acquires momentum. The moderator can ask these prepared questions himself, or give them to another panelist or arrange to have them asked by particular members of the audience.

The moderator, by some lively banter and mild needling, should shut off efforts to make a long speech in the guise of asking or answering a question. This sort of selfish performance by a panelist or person in the audience is another chronic hazard to a succesful panel session.

Livewire Moderator

It is much more important for the moderator to be a livewire M.C. type, with a strong personality and skill with wisecracks, than it is for him to be an expert on the subject under discussion. This is a rule that is almost never recognized and followed. It is no wonder that so many panels and debates are complete flops.

In a question and answer period relying on audience participation there is much to be said for having all the questions planted. This isn't just to be sure the panelists will know the answers. More importantly, it is to avoid the inevitable stupid questions or even worse, questions that are of no interest to anyone except the person doing the asking.

For example, this from a man in the audience at a trade association meeting on unionization problems:

> We have four unions in our plant. Two of them are considering merging. Our lawyer tells us that under Section

309(6)(b) of the National Labor Relations Act, we must take no position on the merger, but our lawyer tells us that under Chapter 13, Section 908.43 of the State Labor Relations Act we are allowed to discuss the merger in our regular company newspaper. However, our newspaper is printed by one of the unions involved in the merger. The question our lawyers are trying to figure out is, if we use another printer will this still be our regular paper under Section 908.43? What do you think?

A few questions like that can sabotage any question and answer program. On paper it seems incredibly stupid and inappropriate and selfish. But questions like this are not at all unusual. Many people can't see beyond their own immediate personal problems and don't put themselves out to contribute to understanding the big picture.

The moderator can't be *too* rough on such jerks. He might reply to the question quoted:

> Two members of our panel are not admitted to the practice of law in this state and therefore the panel feels it is unable to give an opinion.

Or:

> If you will have your lawyers get in touch with the panel so that a split-up of the legal fee can be arranged, our panel will be glad to give an opinion.

Another Rule

Be very cautious about using the various substitutes for speeches before audiences that are likely to be restless, noisy, or inattentive. The audience will quiet down to hear a speech because some who want to listen will "shush" their neighbors who are talking. But in a large hall, such as at a political fund raising banquet, nearly everyone will feel free to talk or even to move around during presentation of a speech received by telephone, or by closed circuit TV. The latter, as well as movies and slides, are additionally bad because the lights must be lowered and restless audiences are like naughty school boys who tend to be noisy in the dark.

I recall an evening which was a notable exception on the use of movies. It was a black tie dinner at the Statler ballroom in Washington to present awards from the Kennedy Foundation for Retarded Children to scientists and doctors who had made notable discoveries in that field. Before each award there was a four- or five-minute film highlighting the awardees' particular experiments and discoveries. Then after the awards and speeches a full length feature film, about the rehabilitation of a retarded boy, was shown.

Impossible?

Normally, yes.

But President Kennedy was there and several of his brothers and sisters and many of the highest government officials.

In addition, the program dealt entirely with a sad, and even somewhat morbid, subject. And it was known by all in the silk stocking audience that the Kennedys were especially interested in the subject because one of the President's sisters has been institutionalized for years.

But if that had been a political dinner in Buffalo and the movies had been of Richard Nixon or Robert Wagner making a speech, the buzz of voices would have turned to a din.

Movies have been used at national political conventions and, aside from the one about President Kennedy's life at the 1964 Atlantic City meeting, have not gone over well. It is not so much because they are so loaded with transparent propaganda; it is more because there is no live human being up there demanding respectful attention. The public is used to skillfully produced film entertainment on TV and in movie theatres. The convention movies about the "accomplishments" (nothing but good) or the "failures" (nothing but bad) of the party in office are as boring to the audience as a movie at a teachers' convention showing a school where every student smiles and studies, and every teacher beams happily.

Use Short *Films*

As I mention elsewhere *short,* well-produced films, can be useful at charity fund raising and award dinners to bring the givers and supporters into closer touch with the need and how it is being met.

Skits are sometimes used at conventions, particularly for gatherings of salesmen. Often they are flops because the participants have not become familiar with their parts and have barely rehearsed so that the performance is often hammy and juvenile.

If a skit is worth giving it is worth the necessary preparation and rehearsal. Speaking parts need not be memorized but the script should be read over several times in advance. It isn't necessary to use participants in the convention as the "actors." There are often local "little theatre" or amateur theatrical groups who will be glad to pick up some money by putting on a skit. Or wives of delegates or home office staff people can be used.

If the message the program arrangers are trying to

get across is simple and uncomplicated, a skit may be just the thing. It shouldn't try to say too much or be too serious. If the participants in the skit are popular and personable members of the organization, they will have a sympathetic audience. But they should not descend to mere clowning and showing off.

Here again it must be remembered that TV and movies have made people sophisticated and blasé about comedy and acting. Even Jackie Gleason found it hard to keep up the pace, so amateurs should proceed with caution.

If a prominent personage is appearing at a convention—for instance, the Secretary of Agriculture at a National Farm Bureau gathering—and if the personage doesn't mind, it is quite effective to hold his press conference in a large room where the convention delegates can listen in. Most people have never attended a real press conference. They will be surprised at the ability of the Secretary to reel off answers to all sorts of tough questions that are thrown at him—never stopping to think that he has probably been asked and has answered most of the same questions at each of his last six sessions with the press.

He may really enjoy press conferences and in that case will not mind at all if others listen in.

XXVIII

Conventions

In this final chapter, I want to stress again that I emphasize humor in speechmaking, not because I think the laughs are an end in themselves, but because a laugh from an audience does show that the speaker has their attention.

I have covered other ways too in which a speaker can avoid being a bore and can make the audience want to listen to him. Some I have mentioned are use of 1. specific examples and suggestions, 2. simple, uncomplicated phraseology, 3. down-to-earth anecdotes and true experiences, 4. good title, 5. natural, conversational manner.

All these are particularly important for convention speeches, because conventions are often just big parties mainly devoted to fun. Besides, there is usually a program of speeches extending over two or three days and "the mind will pay attention only so long as the posterior will endure."

Every year in the United States, there are some 20,000 conventions—national, regional, or state—where at least a substantial percentage of those attending are away from home and staying in hotels and motels. It is estimated that 11 million people register annually at various conventions.

The large conventions, from the standpoint of the speakers, are not just 3-ring circuses, but often 20- and 30-ring circuses. Speaking programs go on simultaneously in a dozen different meeting rooms in several different hotels. The *Wall Street Journal* of August 31, 1964, reported that at the five-day American Chemical Society convention starting that day in Chicago, there were to be 246 program sessions in 34 different meeting rooms. All in all over 1,000 scientific papers were to be presented during the week.

And like nearly all conventions, except those of the W.C.T.U., this was definitely not to be an "all work and no play gathering." An average of 64 cocktail parties a day were scheduled. (Not long ago I read that an Episcopalian clergyman was complaining about too much drinking at a convention of his church.)

This is only to say that the luncheon and dinner speakers at enormous conventions are talking to audiences which have special preoccupations to contend with: too many speeches, taxi problems in moving between hotels, shopping and theater involvements, late sleepers, and cocktails, cocktails, cocktails.

The program chairmen have a special challenge to see that the speakers they have recruited—usually many months in advance—are courteously welcomed, properly housed, appropriately introduced, and most important of all that there is a good crowd on hand when the speech begins.

This can't be left to chance. Too many times I have seen a speaker for a convention section scheduled in Dining Room A at the XYZ Hotel at 12:30 p.m. and so few people show up that it is embarrassing for all concerned. Selling no-refund tickets in advance is one good approach, and the event must be promoted and advertised to stir up interest.

Sales Conventions

Many conventions are put on and paid for by employers for their salesmen. These are especially common in the life insurance business where salesmanship is the lifeblood of the operation. They are also common in the electrical appliance, automobile, and other industries.

Employers always carefully refer to these as "training and educational" meetings in the hope that this will make it possible for each salesman-delegate to have a proper basis for avoiding payment of income tax on the amount spent by the employer for sending him to the convention.

The courts have held that the amount spent by the employer for the salesman's travel and convention expenses is "income" to the salesman if the convention trip is in fact a reward for good sales results. The question then arises whether this "income" may be rendered non-taxable in whole or in part by letting the salesman claim deduction as "ordinary and necessary business expense" for amounts spent on his behalf.

So far courts have been fairly lenient in allowing such deductions by the salesman. For example, here was the schedule of activities for a life insurance sales convention held at Fort Monroe, Virginia:

WEDNESDAY, MAY 16:
 1:30 Arrival
 1:30-5:00 "Renewing old acquaintances and making new acquaintances"
 6:30 Company dinner and water show

THURSDAY, MAY 17:
 7:00-9:30 Breakfast with delegates
 10:00 Meeting (2½ hours)
 Afternoon—No planned activity (Taxpayer played golf)
 8:30 Movie

FRIDAY, MAY 18:
 7:00-8:30 Breakfast with delegates
 9:00 Tour of Williamsburg and Jamestown
 8:30 Bingo

SATURDAY, MAY 19:
 7:00-9:30 Breakfast with delegates
 10:00 Meeting (2½ hours)
 Afternoon Boat Trip
 7:00 President's Banquet and Ball

The courts pointed out that the speeches at the Saturday meeting were on "educational" subjects. The courts concluded that 90 hours were spent by the salesman at the convention and that 50 of these hours, *including the time the salesman spent for sleep,* were devoted to a "business" purpose, i.e., becoming trained and motivated to sell more life insurance. This was on the realistic theory that salesmen "talk shop" when together at conventions.

Expect Instructions

The significance of all this is that speakers asked to be on the program at such meetings should expect to be instructed in advance, by tax conscious company executives, as to what they should say. This may offend the dignity of some speakers. But it is a fact of life at this type of convention where the employer, to advance his own purpose and to satisfy the tax collector, wants everything on the program to help "motivate" his salesmen and buoy up their selling urge.

Those speakers who may balk at accepting instructions on what to say can take heart from the fact that the distinguished Billy Graham doesn't object to this system. He is willing to make speeches "to order."

I listened to him make an incredible speech in Los Angeles, sponsored and paid for by Hubert Eaton of Forest Lawn Cemetery fame, the burden of which was that tax supported colleges and universities were socialistic!

The following is from the dissenting opinion in a tax case involving a life insurance company's sales convention:

> The insidious purpose—here used with no moral overtones of disparagement—of the company's theme on the minds and wills of its captive audience, was exemplified in

the most intense fashion by the Friday luncheon at the Hotel Waldorf-Astoria which ostensibly had no specific relation to selling life insurance. One of the nation's outstanding ministers and public speakers, renowned for his syndicated writings, television and radio appearances, was the luncheon speaker. But even this was not left to chance. The company, by letter, outlined to him the nature of the meeting and suggested that the talk be "of an inspirational nature, along the lines of achievement, success and happiness that can be obtained through proper attitudes of faith and practices of the well-ordered personal life." After discussing the nature of a life insurance agent's work and the essential motivation of genuine service to his clients, management's estimate of the importance of these things was stamped by this conclusion in the letter. "Therefore, the degree of success and satisfaction obtained from his work depends not just entirely upon his knowledge of life insurance, but to a very large degree depends upon his attitudes toward his opportunities and his zeal to excel." It is not surprising that the agency vice president testified of this speech that this speaker "did a better job than I had hoped he would" and that the speaker "did mention something specifically about the work of an insurance man" and "he knew more about it than I did."

There is an amusing true story about Forest Lawn Cemetery with its ridiculous euphemistic gobbledegook and sound effects. After World War II, the English author, Evelyn Waugh, a searing satirist, came to Los Angeles intent upon writing an elaborate spoof of Forest Lawn. He made inquiry at the cemetery's public relations department which did not realize how Waugh wrote and obligingly loaded him with all the gooey details of the mortuary's highly commercial "cheerful undertaker" operation. Waugh obtained everything he wanted and more and in 1948 published *The Loved One* which is one of the most amusing and effective satires ever written.

Hubert Eaton, the head of Forest Lawn, once invited me to a big stag party at the Los Angeles Country Club. The theme of the party was an African safari. The invitation arrived in the form of a 45 rpm phonograph record which started out with assorted jungle roars, groans, screeches, and howls, plus the beating of tom toms. As an example of how the extreme right winger often is unable to see himself as others see him, Eaton's phonograph invitation described him as the "great white hunter." He might better have omitted that. His cemetery prides itself on accepting the remains only of Caucasians!

Two successful salesmen who had never been off Manhattan Island attended a company sales convention in Las Vegas. After the business sessions, they headed for the hotel casino and their luck was phenomenal. At the convention's end they had won so much they had bundles of money in the closet of their hotel room. Sam did not want to fly and Irving did not want to go by train, so they finally decided to take a taxi back to New York City. After their bundles and baggage were jammed into the trunk and 20-dollar tips had been handed around, Sam told Irving to get in the cab.

"No, you get in first," Irving insisted.

"No, you first," said Sam.

"No, Sam. You get in first. I get out at 72nd Street."

Political Conventions

The national political conventions are in most respects a horrible example of things to avoid at big gatherings: dull, repetitious speeches; late starts; empty seats; canned, cut and dried programs with no sparkle and spontaneity. These political conventions should be shortened to three days. They actually don't need to be even that long to transact the necessary work. But a good deal of time is needed for the main business of these and many other conventions: seeing and being seen.

One would think that speakers at these affairs would be sensitive to the reactions of the audience, both live and television. Most people consider these convention speeches trite and tiresome. There is little sparkle and imagination. The speakers yell as though there were no microphones. The man in the street knows, even if the politician doesn't, that a real revolution is needed in political speechmaking.

The same can be said of many other conventions.

With prepared texts and mimeographed handouts, there is little chance for surprise and improvisation to lighten these dull affairs.

Humor provides the best hope for making them enjoyable and holding the interest of the audience.

Professional Organization a Must

A convention must definitely be run by an expert, preferably a real professional. There is just too much to know about and plan to trust to luck and improvisation. The planning of conventions is not directly within the theme of this book. But one of my main points has been that a speaker can do his best only if he is in a good mood, and he can be in a good mood only if the arrangements are handled smoothly so that he does not feel irritated or preoccupied when he comes to the podium.

Even the most sparkling speaker or M.C. cannot be a success if the audience is grouchy because they had to stand in line two hours to register for a hotel room, or because no way has been provided for them to locate friends who are also attending the convention.

The planning for very large conventions may start five or six years in advance, particularly if it is necessary to get control of several thousand hotel rooms. Only a few cities can handle the largest conventions: Chicago, New York City, Atlantic City, Miami Beach, and San Francisco, with Washington about to enter the competition. For a given organization some cities will draw more registrants than others. It is of top importance to come as close as possible on the advance estimate of the number that will attend.

One trouble with many big conventions is that they have too many events. The organization is often divided up into sections by specialities and each section undertakes to run a full-scale program. A smaller number of sessions with top-flight speakers would create more interest.

They tell the story of a man from out of town who accepted an invitation to address an organization which gathered monthly to hear speeches. After he had talked the program chairman offered him a check for $150 as an honorarium. The man declined politely and said he wished to donate his services.

The program chairman's eyes brightened.

"Good," he said. "Then we'll put this in our Improvement Fund?"

"Your Improvement Fund?"

"Yes, we hope to build up enough of a surplus so that next year we can afford to have better speakers!"

That's what we all hope for.

INDEX

A

Absurd, humor of the, 117
Accountants, jokes about, 189-90
Agenda, function of the, 131-33
Alienation of the speaker, 60-61
Alfalfa Club, the, 164, 165
Allusion, humor by, 135-36
American Medical Association, the, 154
Anecdotes, personal, 10-12
Apologetic humor, 19-21
Applause, control of, 165-66
Attention, test for speaker's hold on, 14-15
Attorneys, jokes about, 194
Audience:
college students as, 156
creation of receptive, 7-9
fitting the speaker to the, 38-42
garnering an, 212-14
reading to vs. talking to, 83
size of, fitting speech to, 125-26
using one's, 156-57
Audience participation, 128-29
Audiences:
conservatism of, 43
inattentive, 14
restive, 221-22
Authority, a single source of, 69-70
Axe-grinding, avoidance of, 156-57

B

Back-up man, the, 160-63
Back-up speakers, 51
Bad form, avoidance of, 21-23
Barkley, Alben, 136
Biography, the speaker's, 216
Bishops, jokes about, 188-89
Bohemian Club, the, 173
Bore, characteristics of the, 178-79
Boredom, avoiding the sound of, 83
Boss, the program-planning, 32-33, 168
Brevity, 153
and size of group, 129-30
in speech titles, 171-72
Brower, Charles H., 28
Brown, Pat, 73
Bryan, William Jennings, 155
Buchwald, Art, 117
Buffet dinners, speeches and, 66
Burch, Dean, 10
Business centers, jokes about, 79

C

Canned speeches, 85-87
Catalog of jokes, making a, 72
Chambers of commerce as source of speakers, 48
Children's Aid Society, the, 113
Churches, jokes about, 197-204